Environment and Trade

A Handbook

The United Nations Environment Programme
Division of Technology, Industry and Economics
Economics and Trade Unit
and the
International Institute for Sustainable Development

IISD

INTERNATIONAL INSTITUTE FOR
SUSTAINABLE DEVELOPMENT
INSTITUT INTERNATIONAL DU
DÉVELOPPEMENT DURABLE

United Nations Environment Programme
Division of Technology,
Industry and Economics
Economics and Trade Unit   UNEP

Copyright © 2000 United Nations Environment Programme, International Institute for Sustainable Development
Published by the International Institute for Sustainable Development

Printed in Canada

Copies are available from UNEP and IISD. To order, please contact either of the producers of the handbook:

United Nations Environment Programme
c/o SMI Distribution Services Ltd.
P.O. Box 119, Stevenage
Hartfordshire, England SG1 4TP

Tel.: +44 (1438) 748-111
Fax: +44 (1438) 748-844
E-mail: Anthony@smibooks.com

International Institute for Sustainable Development
161 Portage Avenue East, 6th Floor
Winnipeg, Manitoba
Canada R3B 0Y4

Tel.: +1 (204) 958-7700
Fax: +1 (204) 958-7710
E-mail: info@iisd.ca
Internet: http://iisd.ca/

Copies may also be ordered through IISD's on-line order form at
<http://iisd.ca/about/prodcat/ordering.htm>.

Canadian Cataloguing in Publication Data

Environment and trade: a handbook

ISBN 1-895536-21-9

1. International trade—Environmental aspects.
2. Environmental policy—Economic aspects.
I. United Nations Environment Programme. Division of Technology, Industry and Economics. Economics and Trade Unit.
II. International Institute for Sustainable Development

HF1379.E58 2000   382   C00-920003-7

This publication is printed on recycled paper.

The United Nations Environment Programme

The United Nations Environment Programme (UNEP) is the overall coordinating environmental organization of the United Nations system. Its mission is to provide leadership and encourage partnerships in caring for the environment by inspiring, informing and enabling nations and people to improve their quality of life without compromising that of future generations.

UNEP's Economics and Trade Unit (ETU) is one of the units of the Division of Technology, Industry and Economics (DTIE). Its mission is to enhance capacities of countries, particularly developing countries and countries with economies in transition, to integrate environmental considerations in development planning and macroeconomic policies, including trade policies. The work program of the Unit consists of three main components: economics, trade and financial services. The trade component of the programme focuses on improving countries' understanding of the linkages between trade and environment and enhancing their capacities in developing mutually supportive trade and environment policies, and providing technical input to the trade and environment debate through a transparent and a broad-based consultative process.

For more information, please contact:

Hussein Abaza
Chief, Economics and Trade Unit
Division of Technology, Industry and Economics
United Nations Environment Programme
11–13, chemin des Anémones
CH-1219 Chatelaine/Geneva
Tel.: +41 (22) 917 82 98; 917 81 79
Fax: +41 (22) 917 80 76
E-mail: hussein.abaza@unep.ch
Internet: http://www.unep.ch/etu

The International Institute for Sustainable Development

The International Institute for Sustainable Development is an independent, not-for-profit corporation headquartered in Winnipeg, Canada. IISD's mission is to champion innovation, enabling societies to live sustainably. Established by the governments of Canada and Manitoba, IISD receives financial support from the governments of Canada and Manitoba, other national governments, UN agencies, foundations and the private sector.

IISD's work in trade and sustainable development seeks to find those areas of synergy where trade, environment and development can be mutually beneficial, and to help policy-makers exploit those opportunities. It concentrates on two major themes in its work: reform of trade rules and institutions, and building capacity in developing countries to address the issues of trade and sustainable development. Since 1991 IISD has worked to broaden the terms of the trade-environment debates to encompass the concerns and objectives of developing countries—to make them evolve into debates about trade and sustainable development. To that end in 1994 IISD brought together a group of eminent members of the trade, environment and development communities to produce a framework for addressing the issues in an integrated fashion: the Winnipeg Principles for Trade and Sustainable Development. These principles still serve today as the starting point for the institute's work.

For more information, please contact:

Mark Halle
Director, Trade and Investment
International Institute for Sustainable Development
161 Portage Avenue East, 6th Floor
Winnipeg, Manitoba
Canada R3B 0Y4
Tel.: +1 (204) 958-7700
Fax: +1 (204) 958-7710
E-mail: mhalle@iisd.ca
Internet: http://iisd.ca/trade

"The need to ensure that trade and environment policies are mutually supportive is more pressing today than ever before. However, successful integration of these policies can only be achieved through a constructive dialogue based on far broader awareness and understanding of the complex interlinkages between trade and our environment."

Dr. Klaus Töpfer,
Executive Director, UNEP

Preface

All around the world, the growth and liberalization of international trade is changing the way we live and work. At $6 trillion a year, trade flows and the rules that govern them are a massive force for economic, environmental and social change. International trade is becoming an increasingly important driver of economic development, as it has been expanding at almost twice the pace of total global economic activity for the past 15 years. A growing number of developing countries look to trade and investment as a central part of their strategies for development, and trade considerations are increasingly important in shaping economic policy in all developed countries, too.

The handbook has been developed to highlight the relationship between environment and trade. The primary aim is to foster a broader understanding of these interlinkages to enable governments to develop practical approaches to integrating these policies. It is possible, but by no means automatic, that trade and environmental policies should support each other in achieving their objectives. Close integration of these policies is necessary to maximize the benefits that trade can bring to increase human welfare and economic development more sustainably.

The handbook is aimed mainly at those with some knowledge about trade, environment or development, but not expert on the intersection of the three. It is also a practical reference tool for policy-makers and practitioners. But the target audience is not just government policy-makers; the media and public may also find it useful. The handbook uses clear language and a minimum of jargon to foster a greater understanding by all elements of civil society.

This handbook should help us understand how trade can affect the environment, for better and for worse, and how environmental concern can work through the trading system to foster or frustrate development, in both rich and poor countries. It is critical to ensure that trade's potential for growth and development does, in fact, lead to environmentally sustainable development. Broader understanding and awareness of these linkages will then be the foundation on which fair and environmentally sustainable policies and trade flows are built.

The handbook is also available in a continually updated Web version at both **http://www.unep.ch/etu** and **http://iisd.ca/trade/handbook**. Here, readers can link to on-line articles and analyses that go into greater depth on the themes covered in the print version. The Web version will also have other resources, such as a compendium of trade and environment disputes and links to other sites of interest.

Acknowledgements

This handbook is the product of many hands. The inspiration and energy for the project came from both the Economics and Trade Unit of UNEP's Division of Technology, Industry and Economics, and IISD's team working on trade and sustainable development. Jacqueline Aloisi de Larderel, Hussein Abaza, Charles Arden-Clarke, Eugenia Nuñez, Sophie Forster and Mariko Hara led the project for UNEP and Aaron Cosbey from IISD was the project manager. The contributors were Aaron Cosbey, Mark Halle, Howard Mann, Konrad von Moltke, Marie-Claire Segger, Jason Switzer, Sarah Richardson, Tom Rotherham and Tina Winqvist. Joe Petrik served as editor and Rae Fenwick and Don Berg worked on design and layout. Pat Gallimore and Valentina Kaltchev provided administrative support.

Thanks are due to a number of generous and capable reviewers. These include Richard Blackhurst, Duncan Brack, Terry Collins, Veena Jha and Matthew Stilwell, who read and commented on two drafts of the document in their capacity as the project's advisory group. They also include Christian Friis Bach, Richard Ballhorn, Mike Beale, Steve Charnovitz, Kilian Delbrück, Michael J. Finger, Margaret Flaherty, Bill Glanville, Shahrukh Rafi Khan, Ricardo Meléndez-Ortiz, Mark Ritchie, Ye Ruqiu, Risa Schwartz, Sabrina Shaw, Trân Van Thinh and Scott Vaughan, who reviewed various drafts of the document in their capacity as the project's peer review group. While their help was invaluable in shaping this book, neither the reviewers nor the organizations they represent should bear responsibility for the final product.

Table of Contents

Abbreviations

CBD	Convention on Biological Diversity
CEC	Commission for Environmental Cooperation
CFCs	chlorofluorocarbons
CITES	Convention on International Trade in Endangered Species of Wild Fauna and Flora
COP	Conference of Parties
CTE	Committee on Trade and Environment
DSB	Dispute Settlement Body
DSM	dispute settlement mechanism
DSU	Dispute Settlement Understanding
EU	European Union
FAO	Food and Agriculture Organization
FCCC	Framework Convention on Climate Change
FDI	foreign direct investment
GATS	General Agreement on Trade in Services
GATT	General Agreement on Tariffs and Trade
GDP	gross domestic product
GMO	genetically modified organism
IEA	international environmental agreement
ISO	International Organization for Standardization
LCA	life cycle analysis
LMO	living genetically modified organism
MAI	Multilateral Agreement on Investment
MEA	multilateral environmental agreement
Mercosur	*Mercado Común del Sur* (Southern Common Market: Argentina, Brazil, Paraguay, Uruguay)
MFN	most-favoured nation
NAFTA	North American Free Trade Agreement (Canada, Mexico, United States)

NGO	non-governmental organization
OECD	Organization for Economic Co-operation and Development
PCBs	polychlorinated biphenyls
PIC	The Rotterdam Convention on the Prior Informed Consent Procedure for Certain Hazardous Chemicals and Pesticides in International Trade
POPs	Convention on the Control of Persistent Organic Pollutants
PPMs	process and production methods
PVP	plant variety protection
R&D	research and development
SPS	Agreement on Sanitary and Phytosanitary Measures
SRM	standards-related measures
TBT	Agreement on Technical Barriers to Trade
TRIMs	Agreement on Trade-Related Investment Measures
TRIPS	Agreement on Trade-Related Aspects of Intellectual Property Rights
UNCED	United Nations Conference on Environment and Development
UNCTAD	United Nations Conference on Trade and Development
UNEP	United Nations Environment Programme
UPOV	International Convention for the Protection of New Varieties of Plants
WIPO	World Intellectual Property Organization
WTO	World Trade Organization

−1−
Introduction

1.1   Global trends

OUR WORLD HAS SEEN FUNDAMENTAL AND PERVASIVE CHANGE in the last 50 years. National economies are increasingly integrated in a global economic structure where all the elements needed to produce a final good or service—production of inputs, design, assembly, management, marketing, savings for investment—may be sourced from around the globe in a system held together by powerful communications and information technologies. The trend toward globalization has been driven in part by these new technologies, and in part by reduced barriers to international trade and investment flows. The result has been a steady increase in the importance of international trade in the global economy: in the last 50 years, while the global economy quintupled, world trade grew by a factor of 14.

Another important trend is increasing inequity; the benefits of growth have been unevenly spread. Although average global income now exceeds $5,000 US per person a year, 1.3 billion people still survive on incomes of less than a dollar a day. The world's three richest people have a combined wealth greater than the GDPs of the 48 least developed countries. And the growing inequality between and within nations shows no signs of abating.

In the last 50 years, the world has also seen enormous environmental change. Global carbon dioxide emissions have quadrupled, and the steady increase in nitrogen releases from cars and fertilizers is creating deserts of lifelessness in our oceans and lakes. One-quarter of the world's fish stocks are depleted, and another 44 per cent are being fished at their biological limits. In 30 years, if current trends continue, two-thirds of the world will live with "water stress"—having less than 1,000 litres of water per person a year. Daily, 25,000 people die because of diseases caused by poor water management. A quarter of the world's mammal species are at significant risk of extinction. Such environmental damage has been driven at least in part by our increasing numbers—population has increased about 2^1/2 times since 1950, to over 6 billion in 1999.

The institutions for addressing such problems have also evolved. In the last 15 years alone 11 major multilateral environmental agreements have entered into force, dealing with such issues as ozone depletion, transport of hazardous waste, and migratory species. At the regional or bilateral level roughly a thousand more have entered into force, constituting an enormous and complex body of environmental law. At the national level, regulators have moved from blanket "command and control" solutions to a mixed bag of tools that includes market-based incentives such as pollution charges and taxes. For select problems the result has been marked by environmental improvement, but for many more the discouraging trends continue.

1.2   Environment and trade linkages

These trends are not isolated; they are fundamentally related. Much environmental damage is due to the increased scale of global economic activity. International trade constitutes a growing portion of that growing scale, making it increasingly important as a driver of environmental change. As economic globalization proceeds and the global nature of many environmental problems becomes more evident, there is bound to be friction between the multilateral systems of law governing both.

This book aims to shed light on the area where these broad trends interact—on the physical, legal and institutional linkages between international trade and the environment. Two fundamental truths about the relationship should become clear in the process:

- The links between trade and the environment are multiple, complex and important.

- Trade liberalization is—of itself—neither necessarily good nor bad for the environment. Its effects on the environment in fact depend on the extent to which environment and trade goals can be made complementary and mutually supportive. A positive outcome requires appropriate supporting economic and environmental policies.

At the most basic level, trade and the environment are related because all economic activity is based on the environment. It is the basis for all basic inputs (metals and minerals, forests and fisheries), and for the energy needed to process them. It also receives the waste products of economic activity. Trade, in turn, is affected by environmental concerns, since exporters must respond to market demands for greener goods. These physical and economic linkages are explored in chapter 4.

At another level, environment and trade represent two distinct bodies of international law. Trade law is embodied in such structures as the World Trade Organization and regional trade agreements. Environmental law is embodied

2

in the various multilateral environmental agreements, the regional agreements and as national and subnational regulations. It is inevitable that these two systems of law should interact. International environmental law increasingly defines how countries will structure their economic activities (parties to the United Nations Framework Convention on Climate Change, for example, have pledged to restructure their economies to cut greenhouse gas emissions), and international trade law increasingly defines how countries should make their domestic laws and policies in areas such as intellectual property rights, investment policy and environmental protection. These legal linkages are explored in chapter 5.

Finally, a host of institutional questions are born of the trade-environment relationship. What institutions might help ensure that trade and environmental policies are mutually supportive? Where and how should disputes be settled? Should there be environmental impact assessment of trade agreements and trade policies? What role should the public have? These questions are examined in chapter 6.

Before delving into the linkages between trade and the environment, we take a basic look at the structure, goals and principles of the international system of environmental management in chapter 2, and the multilateral system of trade rules in chapter 3.

1.3   Differing perspectives

People come to the trade-environment debates from many different backgrounds. The various assumptions and worldviews they start with, and their different technical languages, can be important obstacles to meaningful dialogue and solutions.

People understand the issues through three common perspectives—that of trade, environment and development. Of course, these are not mutually exclusive—many people understand all three. What follows are crude stereotypes of each perspective, but ones that help illustrate the challenge of finding policies that simultaneously support the objectives of trade, environment and development.

The trade perspective

- Trade creates the wealth that could be used to increase human well-being.

- But most national governments answer too directly to national industries, and will try to preserve domestic markets for these industries, keeping foreign competitors at bay.

- In doing so, governments make their citizens worse off: domestic firms become inefficient, domestic consumers pay higher prices, and more efficient foreign firms are shut out.

- The best protection is a strong system of rules against such behaviour, such as WTO rules, by which all countries abide.

- Even after signing such agreements, countries will look for loopholes. Banning or restricting goods on environmental grounds may be one such loophole.

- Trade can actually be good for the environment, since it creates wealth that can be used for environmental improvement, and the efficiency gains from trade can mean fewer resources used and less waste produced.

The environmental perspective

- The status quo seriously threatens the earth's ecosystems.

- But most national governments answer too directly to national industries, and will try to protect them against "costly" environmental demands.

- In doing so, governments make their citizens worse off: domestic firms make profits, but the public subsidizes them by paying the costs of environmental degradation.

- One way to avoid these problems is a strong system of rules spelling out clearly how the environment shall be protected, at the national and international levels.

- Even after such rules are in place, governments and industry will look to scuttle them. Trade rules forbidding certain types of environmental regulations may be one way to do so.

- Trade means more goods produced and thus in many cases more environmental damage. The wealth created by trade will not necessarily result in environmental improvements.

The development perspective

- Over one-fifth of the world's population live in absolute poverty, most of them in developing countries, and the gap between the rich and poor countries continues to widen. Developing countries' top priority should be reducing that poverty and narrowing that gap.

- Openness to trade and investment may be a key way to do so, by increasing exports, though the links between openness and economic growth are not automatic.

- But rich countries protect their industries with subsidies, special trade rules and tariff systems that hurt developing country exporters.

- The best solution is a strong set of multilateral rules against such behaviour, but current WTO rules are too deeply influenced by the powerful trading nations, and liberalization has selectively benefited sectors of interest to developed countries.

- Over time, as such behaviour is outlawed by trade rules, rich countries will look for new ways to keep foreign competition out of their markets. Banning or restricting goods on environmental grounds may be one of those ways.

- Demands that poor countries comply with rich country environmental standards are unfair, particularly if they are not accompanied by technical or financial assistance. Priorities differ; for example, in many poor countries clean water is paramount. And rich countries often caused most of the environmental damage in the first place.

Suggested readings

Global trends

United Nations Development Programme. *Human development report*, 1998. New York: UNDP. <http://www.undp.org/hdro/98.htm>.

United Nations Environment Programme. *GEO-2000*. London: Earthscan Publications Ltd., 1999. <http://www.unep.org/geo2000/>.

Environment and trade linkages

Nordstrom, Hakan and Scott Vaughan. *Trade and environment* (special studies #4). Geneva: WTO, 1999.

OECD. *The environmental effects of trade*. Paris: OECD, 1994.

Differing perspectives

Gonzales, Aimée and David Stone. *Towards sustainable trade: For people and the environment*. Gland: WWF International, 1999. <http://www.panda.org/resources/publications/sustainability/wto-papers/build.html>.

International Institute for Sustainable Development. *Trade and sustainable development principles*. Winnipeg: IISD, 1994. <http://iisd.ca/trade/princip2.htm>.

–2–
International environmental management

2.1 Origins

THE MODERN SYSTEM OF INTERNATIONAL ENVIRONMENTAL MANAGEMENT dates to the 1972 United Nations Conference on the Human Environment, held in Stockholm. Several international environmental agreements, in particular some on marine pollution, predate the Stockholm Conference but this first major environmental event triggered a flurry of activity at national and international levels, as countries and other international organizations responded to the emerging challenges of environmental management at all levels. The Stockholm Conference also pioneered new forms of public participation in a United Nations conference, establishing links between the formal process and the informal parallel NGO process.

The Stockholm Conference led to the establishment of the United Nations Environment Programme, headquartered in Nairobi, Kenya. UNEP was to act as a catalyst for the environment in the United Nations system, but its means were modest compared with the dimensions of its task. Over the years, however, UNEP has launched a significant number of international agreements, and today has administrative responsibility for seven major conventions as well as many regional agreements. It has also acted as the environmental conscience of the United Nations system.

It soon became obvious that the Stockholm Conference's focus on the environment without due concern for development was not enough for the long-term advancement of the international environmental agenda. In 1985 the United Nations established the World Commission on Environment and Development, which issued its report, *Our common future*, in 1987. This report first articulated the concept of sustainable development systematically (see Box 2-1). This in turn became the basis for a major review of all international environmental activities in the United Nations through the United Nations Conference on Environment and Development, held in 1992 in Rio de Janeiro, Brazil. UNCED articulated an ambitious program of sustainable development, contained in the final Conference document, known as Agenda 21. The Rio Conference helped establish the United Nations Commission on Sustainable Development and reaffirmed the role of the Global Environment Facility, thus widening the organizational basis for the environment and sustainable development within the United Nations system. UNCED was the fulcrum on which states were able to conclude the Framework Convention on Climate Change and the Convention on Biological Diversity, after short and very intense negotiations. UNCED also pioneered innovative ways for the public to participate in intergovernmental processes.

Box 2-1: Sustainable development according to Brundtland

Sustainable development goes further than just concern for the environment. It aims to improve human conditions, but seeks to achieve it in an environmentally sustainable way. According to the "Brundtland Commission" report, *Our common future*, sustainable development is:

Development that meets the needs of the present without compromising the ability of future generations to meet their own needs. It contains within it two key concepts:

- The concept of 'needs', in particular the essential needs of the world's poor, to which overriding priority should be given; and

- The idea of limitations imposed by the state of technology and social organization on the environment's ability to meet present and future needs.

Source: World Commission on Environment and Development. Our common future. Oxford: Oxford University Press, 1987.

2.2 Principles

The structure of international environmental regimes must reflect the structure of the problem being addressed. A regime that protects biodiversity needs to use different tools, draw on different constituencies and have different institutional arrangements than one that protects the oceans from oil pollution, or one that manages international trade in endangered species. Nevertheless, most environmental regimes have come to respect several fundamental principles and to articulate them through their institutions. Many of these principles were laid out in the Rio Declaration on Environment and Development, another product of UNCED 1992. Six key principles are described below.

Prevention. It is generally expensive, difficult or impossible to repair environmental damage once it has occurred, so it is better to avoid such damage in the first place. This apparently self-evident fact has significant practical implications, since it requires action before there is any damage; that is, it requires action based on the *possibility* of damage.

Precaution. Calculating the possibility of damage is a difficult task, because our knowledge of ecological and environmental processes is frequently rudimentary at best, and is based on an evolving foundation of scientific research. Unfortunately, science does not always provide clear guidance on the measures that may be needed, so we are often faced with the task of making policy in the face of uncertainty. As articulated in the Rio Declaration, the precautionary principle states that lack of conclusive scientific evidence does not justify inaction, particularly when the consequences of inaction may be devastating or when the costs of action are negligible.

Subsidiarity. The linkages between individuals and the global consequences of their actions are a major challenge to the organization of environmental management. In particular it means that rules developed at one level—for example in international regimes—must be adapted to conditions in a wide variety of regional or local environments. The principle of subsidiarity calls for decision-making and responsibility to fall to the lowest level of government or political organization that can effectively take action.

Common but differentiated responsibility. Many environmental regimes require the participation of numerous countries, both rich and poor. But not all countries carry an equal responsibility for past environmental damage, and different countries have different resources at their disposal. So while the parties to environmental regimes all acknowledge common responsibility for the environment, they also work to develop differentiated responsibilities for addressing environmental problems.

Openness. Openness has two elements: transparency and public participation in policy-making. Both are necessary for good environmental management because protecting the environment requires the participation of literally countless people in many locations. Most environmental regimes are highly open, making use of environmental organizations, the media, and the Internet to communicate to the public. Many allow non-governmental organizations to participate in the discussions and negotiations of their provisions.

Polluter-pays principle. The polluter-pays principle was first propounded by the OECD in 1972. At that time it simply said that polluters should have to bear the full cost of meeting environmental regulations and standards. No subsidies should be given to help in this process. It has since evolved to become a broader principle of cost internalization—polluters should pay the full cost of the environmental damage that their activities produce. Of course, much of that cost will be passed along to consumers in the price of the goods involved, but this then discourages consumption of more pollution-intensive goods.

2.3   National environmental management

At the country level these principles are put into practice through a variety of means, including the following:

- Species and habitat conservation measures

- Environmental taxes and charges

- Negotiated voluntary agreements

- Deposit and refund, or take-back, schemes

- Restrictions on certain goods and practices

At the basis of most of these measures, and of the greatest relevance to the environment-trade interface, are environmental standards—particularly those imposed on traded goods. There are many types of environmental standards along the pathway of a product from extracting raw materials through manufacture, transport, trade, sale, use and disposal. They can be grouped under five headings.

Environmental quality standards seek to describe the state of the environment. Environmental standards can be concentrations of certain substances in the air, water or soil. They can be "critical loads," a level of deposition of pollutants below which some elements of the environment are not damaged. They can be population standards requiring the protection of certain species that have become threatened or endangered.

Emission standards identify the amount of certain substances a facility may emit. Emission standards can have a significant impact on production processes that are regulated, since it is generally better to avoid producing pollutants than to capture them at the end of the production process, creating a waste stream that must in turn be managed.

Product standards specify certain characteristics that are deemed necessary to avoid environmental harm from the use or disposal of products. For example, the use of lead in household paints has been banned because some of that toxic heavy metal is likely to reach the environment and pose a hazard, and chlorofluorocarbons have been banned from use in aerosols because they destroy the stratospheric ozone layer. Product standards are frequently used to protect human health.

Process and production standards specify how products are to be produced and what kinds of impact they may have on the environment. Standards based on process and production methods take on significance in international trade that they completely lack at the domestic level. Applied to traded goods, they amount to the regulating country setting standards on economic activities in the country of production.

Performance standards require certain actions, such as environmental assessment, which are expected to improve environmental management.

It is possible to combine all of these measurements and standards when ana-lyzing the full impact of a single product—to consider all the environmental impacts of a product's production, use and disposal, and to combine them in a single life cycle analysis. An LCA can be used to identify opportunities to reduce environmental impacts, or to compare the environmental impacts of otherwise "like" products—for example, cloth diapers and disposable diapers, or different kinds of beverage containers. LCAs by definition look at a large number of categories of environmental impacts—for example, water and energy use, and release of various pollutants. The problem in comparing products lies in adding up the various types of impacts—and deciding how to weight them—to calculate an overall measure of environmental impact.

The overall effect of all these standards is to force producers, traders and con-sumers to consider the environmental impact of the economic decisions they take; in other words, they must begin to internalize the external environmen-tal costs in their calculations. It is of course possible to achieve the same goal by using market-based instruments such as taxes, charges, tradable permits or subsidies. The advantage of such instruments is that they are generally more economically efficient. Their drawback is that, like standards, they require pre-cisely articulated environmental goals as well as constant monitoring to ensure that the desired results are being achieved. It is important to recognize, how-ever, that all of these measures, both regulatory and market-based, result in structural economic change as environmentally desirable activities are favoured and environmentally undesirable ones disadvantaged.

This large number and variety of standards, usually used in combination rather than alone, create an extensive management structure in which each standard complements the other, and few if any are effective just by them-selves. They all have economic implications, creating potential problems for the trading system, which has thus far dealt mostly with product standards.

2.4 Multilateral environmental agreements

2.4.1 Structure

Over the past 20 years, an extraordinary number of international environ-mental agreements have been concluded. More than 200 multilateral envi-ronmental agreements—defined in this book as those involving more than two countries—are known to exist. Some of these are global treaties, open to any country. The number of bilateral agreements is unknown, but is thought to be well in excess of a thousand. The result is an international structure for environmental management that was not premeditated, and that reflects the extraordinary diversity of issues and interests involved.

Very few MEAs actually regulate trade or contain trade provisions. Of the 20 or so that do, even fewer are of notable significance to the environment-trade interface. Seven of the most important are discussed in greater detail below.

Box 2-2: Key MEAs with trade provisions

- Convention on International Trade in Endangered Species of Wild Fauna and Flora (CITES)—1975

- Montreal Protocol on Substances that Deplete the Stratospheric Ozone Layer—1987

- Basel Convention on the Control of Transboundary Movement of Hazardous Wastes and their Disposal—1992

- Convention on Biological Diversity—1993

- Framework Convention on Climate Change (FCCC)—1994

- Rotterdam Convention on the Prior Informed Consent Procedure for Certain Hazardous Chemicals and Pesticides in International Trade (PIC)—1998

- Cartagena Protocol on Biosafety—2000

(Dates indicate entry into force, except for the PIC Convention and the Cartagena Protocol, which have not yet entered into force. Here, the dates refer to the completion of negotiations.)

Increasingly, the complex of institutions and organizations that develop around international environmental agreements are referred to as "regimes," expressing the reality that they involve a number of constituencies and actors, and no longer reflect the dynamics of power between sovereign states alone. The rules governing these regimes differ from one to another reflecting the provisions of the relevant agreement. But all draw on customary international law and a range of practices and principles that have become widely accepted.

The international structure of environmental management is extremely dynamic. The various regimes address a wide variety of issues, ranging from toxic substances to the protection of elephants, from air pollution to biodiversity. As well, they must respond to changing scientific information about the environment, changing perceptions of the significance of this information, and the constant feedback from the successes and failures of the measures adopted in support of their objectives.

2.4.2 The principal MEAs

This handbook defines MEAs as those agreements with more than two parties—that is, multilateral is anything bigger than bilateral. The word has taken on a slightly different meaning for the trade community, for whom "multilateral" has come to mean "global." Below are the MEAs that are particularly relevant to trade regimes.

The Convention on International Trade in Endangered Species. The earliest of the key MEAs, CITES was drawn up in 1973 and entered into force two years later. CITES seeks to control trade in endangered species and their parts, as well as products made from such species. Three annexes list species identified by the Conference of Parties (on scientific advice) as being endangered to various extents. It establishes trade controls, ranging from a complete ban to a partial licensing system. CITES has long been known for the unusually active participation of non-governmental organizations—scientific and advocacy organizations in particular—in its deliberations. (146 parties)

The Vienna Convention on Substances that Deplete the Stratospheric Ozone Layer, with the Montreal Protocol. The Montreal Protocol establishes a regime of control for several classes of industrial chemicals now known to harm the stratospheric ozone layer. The result has been a ban on the production and use of several of them, together with severe limitations on others. It has successfully implemented the principle of precaution, by acting before the availability of clear scientific evidence, and that of common and differentiated responsibility, by establishing a fund to assist developing countries in their transition away from dependency on controlled substances. Its principal enforcement tool—apart from continuing public pressure—is the control of trade in ozone-depleting substances and trade in products containing controlled substances. It included the possibility of imposing controls on trade in products produced with (but no longer containing) controlled substances, but the parties have not considered it necessary to implement such controls. (Vienna Convention: 173 parties; Montreal Protocol: 172 parties)

The Basel Convention on the Control of Transboundary Movement of Hazardous Wastes and their Disposal. The Basel Convention resulted from the concern of developing countries, particularly in Africa, that they could become the dumping ground for hazardous wastes that could no longer be disposed of in the developed world. Developing countries and non-governmental organizations have continued to play a significant role in developing the regime. The Basel Convention has been marked by disputes over the most appropriate strategy for controlling the movement of hazardous waste (regional bans versus prior informed consent) and the technical difficulty in establishing unambiguous distinctions between wastes and materials for recycling. Parties have adopted amendments banning the export of hazardous waste from mainly OECD to non-OECD countries. (131 parties, 3 signatories, not ratified)

Convention on Biological Diversity. Opened for signature at the Rio Conference, the Convention's objective is conserving biological diversity, the sustainable use of its components and the fair and equitable sharing of the benefits arising from the use of genetic resources. The Convention has not been easy to operationalize. The very concept of "biodiversity" is a research construct developed in the past 20 years to better help us understand the natural environment. Protecting a research construct, as opposed to something tangible such as a species or specific habitat, is not a straightforward exercise. Potential conflicts between the CBD and the WTO TRIPS Agreement are discussed in section 5.7.1. (135 parties, 12 signatories, not ratified)

Framework Convention on Climate Change. The FCCC, adopted at the Rio Conference in 1992, is grappling with the most complex of all environmental issues, and the one with greatest potential for economic impacts. Since greenhouse gas emissions can rarely be limited with technical, "end-of-pipe" technologies, the principal strategy of the FCCC must be to change the pattern of future investment in favour of activities that generate less greenhouse gases. In December 1997 the Kyoto Protocol was adopted. It created two classes of countries—those with greenhouse gas limitation commitments and those without—and several institutions governing their relations. Although neither the FCCC nor the Kyoto Protocol includes trade measures, it is highly likely that the parties, in fulfilling their Kyoto obligations, will adopt trade-restrictive policies and measures. (180 parties)

Rotterdam Convention on the Prior Informed Consent (PIC) Procedure for Certain Hazardous Chemicals and Pesticides in International Trade. Many domestically banned or severely limited goods are traded internationally. For years there was controversy over the procedures to ensure that the appropriate authorities in the importing country were informed promptly. Indeed, a GATT working group devoted several years of negotiation to this topic, without achieving a generally acceptable result. UNEP (responsible for arrangements for managing potentially toxic substances) and the Food and Agriculture Organization (concerned with pesticide use) had a strong interest in developing a uniform system of notification. This needed to offer adequate assurance that information would be provided quickly, but also that it would reach the necessary authorities when needed. And it needed to create a system that permitted developing countries to stop the import of certain substances if they felt a need to do so. This goal has been served by the Rotterdam Convention. (62 signatories)

Cartagena Protocol on Biosafety. Cartagena is a Protocol to the CBD, covering trade in most forms of living genetically modified organisms and the risks it may present to biodiversity. It creates an advanced informed agreement system for LMOs destined to be introduced to the environment (such as micro-organisms and seeds), and a less complex system for monitoring those destined for use as food, animal feed or processing. It sets out a procedure for countries to decide whether to restrict imports of LMOs, spelling out, for example, the type of risk assessment that must be carried out. In allowing such decisions to be taken even where the risks are unknown, the Cartagena Protocol operationalizes the precautionary principle perhaps more clearly than any other international agreement to date. Opened for signature in May 2000, it will enter into force when ratified by 50 countries.

Emerging Regimes. Several other international environmental regimes exist, which are still being negotiated, or which are likely to remain based on a less formal understanding between the interested parties. The Convention on Persistent Organic Pollutants has been under negotiation for several years and is expected to be concluded by the end of 2000. Like the Montreal Protocol, the POPs Convention will establish an international regime for the control and, in many cases, the banning of certain pollutants that persist in the environment and can accumulate in the food chain, or that are suspected of disrupting hormones—chemicals known as endocrine disruptors. The *international forest regime* remains controversial and poorly articulated, and most observers doubt that it will coalesce into a multilateral agreement in the near future. We may yet see a private *regime for sustainable fisheries* emerge, the result of collaboration between producers and environmental non-governmental organizations on labelling for sustainable practices. Both of these regimes will be highly relevant for trade, since both involve widely traded commodities.

2.4.3 Implementation and dispute settlement

International environmental regimes involve complex interactions between the parties, their subnational jurisdictions, their citizens and, sometimes, other stakeholders. In practice it often takes several rounds of negotiation before an effective regime emerges. Even then, implementing an MEA at the national level and monitoring its progress at the international level are not simple matters. Among other things they require continual adjustment of the regime—the result of intensive further research on the environmental problem, and on the regime's effectiveness—and of public debate on the results of the research.

International environmental regimes are based on consent. Only the PIC Convention has an elaborate dispute settlement structure, reflecting the fact that it is designed primarily to manage trade in certain hazardous substances rather than protect a specific environmental resource. It is widely recognized that coercion is not a sound basis for environmental policy. Therefore, just as countries use criminal penalties to enforce environmental laws only in cases of extreme disregard, so too do international environmental regimes use coercive dispute settlement only on rare occasions. Most of these cases tend to be disputes over shared waters in regional or bilateral agreements.

Transparency and participation are arguably the most important implementation tools of international environmental regimes but implementation may need the help of an arm's-length agency. Since NGOs can go where governments sometimes fear to tread, they can be critical of countries' internal implementation of MEAs and exert pressure on their own governments for good faith compliance. Scientifically based assessments of environmental developments provide the foundation for most of these agreements, and all of this activity depends on a free flow of information and ready access to decision-making in the regime.

2.4.4 Trade measures in MEAs

It was noted earlier that trade measures in MEAs are uncommon, occurring in roughly one-tenth of all agreements. But those that exist may have important effects on international trade flows. The trade measures found in five MEAs are described in Box 2-3.

Box 2-3: Trade measures in selected MEAs

The Basel Convention: Parties may only export a hazardous waste to another party that has not banned its import and that consents to the import in writing. Parties may not import from or export to a non-party. They are also obliged to prevent the import or export of hazardous wastes if they have reason to believe that the wastes will not be treated in an environmentally sound manner at their destination.

The Convention on International Trade in Endangered Species: CITES bans commercial international trade in an agreed list of endangered species. It also regulates and monitors (by use of permits, quotas and other restrictive measures) trade in other species that might become endangered.

The Montreal Protocol: The Protocol lists certain substances as ozone depleting, and bans all trade in those substances between parties and non-parties. Similar bans may be implemented against parties as part of the Protocol's non-compliance procedure. The Protocol also contemplates allowing import bans on products made with, but not containing, ozone-depleting substances—a ban based on process and production methods.

The Rotterdam PIC Convention: Parties can decide, from the Convention's agreed list of chemicals and pesticides, which ones they cannot manage safely and, therefore, will not import. When trade in the controlled substances does take place, labelling and information requirements must be followed. Decisions taken by the parties must be trade neutral—if a party decides not to consent to imports of a specific chemical, it must also stop domestic production of the chemical for domestic use, as well as imports from any non-party.

The Cartagena Protocol on Biosafety: Parties may restrict the import of some living genetically modified organisms as part of a carefully specified risk management procedure. Living GMOs that will be intentionally released to the environment are subject to an advance informed agreement procedure, and those destined for use as food, feed or processing must be accompanied by documents identifying them.

Why do some environmental agreements incorporate trade measures? The explanation will vary according to the circumstances of the agreement. But there are at least four reasons why trade measures are sometimes considered necessary:

1. *Regulatory frameworks.* Participants in a market need to be confident that all others face comparable regulatory constraints—and that these are being implemented properly. Some constraints reflect the economic and social choices of consumers, so such constraints can be viewed as part of the normal conditions of competition. Others reflect scientifically based environmental imperatives and must be respected to avoid severe and irreversible damage, irrespective of other priorities. Sorting out which constraints are mandatory for all market participants and which can be viewed as optional is one of the major tasks facing trade and environmental communities alike.

2. *Containment.* Sometimes, the practical requirements of administering environmental market disciplines impose a need to maintain certain borders. For example, imposing size limits on lobsters that are caught generally protects lobster stocks, but these limitations are enforced not on the boat but in the marketplace. In practice lobsters mature faster in warmer waters, so a smaller size limit achieves the same conservation goal. This may seem like a classic case of comparative advantage but a trade panel has ruled that the United States may exclude smaller Canadian lobsters from its market because it could not maintain an essential conservation discipline without such a ban.

Similar reasoning can apply to hazardous wastes or toxic substances, both of which become increasingly difficult to control the further they are transported.

3. **Controlling markets.** Some products may have high demand but meeting that demand may destroy the resources on which they are based. It can prove difficult or even impossible to ensure that the scarcity value of these products is adequately reflected in the price— and that the associated profits are distributed in a way that promotes rather than undermines conservation. Under these circumstances an international structure of market control is required. This is the logic behind CITES and plays a significant role in the CBD.

4. **Ensuring compliance.** The threat of imposing limits on trade with non-parties can be an effective tool for securing greater compliance with MEAs than might otherwise be so. This was done effectively in the Montreal Protocol. Clearly, it is important to ensure that the limits are neither arbitrary nor disproportionate; that is, they cannot restrict a substantial amount of trade to address a relatively small environmental problem.

Suggested readings

Origins

UNCED collection. Centre for International Earth Science Information Network, Columbia University, New York. <http://www.ciesin.org/datasets/unced/unced.html>.

UNEP home page. UNEP. <http://www.unep.org/>.

World Commission on Environment and Development. *Our common future.* Oxford: Oxford University Press, 1987.

Principles

Hunter, David, James Salzman and Durwood Zaelke. *International environmental law and policy* (esp. chapter 7: "Principles and concepts in international environmental law"). New York: Foundation Press, 1998.

Hunter, David, Julia Sommer and Scott Vaughan. *Concepts and principles of international environmental law* (environment and trade series #2). Geneva: UNEP, 1994. <gopher://gopher.undp.org:70/11/ungophers/unep/publications/monographs/mon_02>.

OECD. *Environmental principles and concepts* (OCDE/GD(95)124). Paris: OECD, 1995.
<http://www.olis.oecd.org/olis/1995doc.nsf/linkto/ocde-gd(95)124>.

National environmental management

World Bank. *Five years after Rio: Innovations in environmental policy.* Washington, D.C.: World Bank, 1997.
<http://wbln0018.worldbank.org/environment/EEI.nsf/3dc00e2e46240235 85256713005a1d4a/a5c925162bbd655e8525671c00774d99?OpenDocument>.

MEAs

Linkages: A multimedia resource for environment and development policy makers. IISD. <http://www.iisd.ca/>.

UNEP. *Environmental legal instruments (MEAs).* UNEP.
<http://www.unep.org/unep/conv.htm>.

Vaughan, Scott and Ali Dehlavi. *Policy effectiveness and MEAs* (environment and trade series #17). Geneva: UNEP, 1998.
<http://www.unep.ch/eteu/trade/TRADE17.html>.

von Moltke, Konrad. *International environmental management, trade regimes and sustainability.* Winnipeg: IISD, 1996.
<http://iisd.ca/pdf/envmanage.pdf>.

–3–
The basics of the WTO

THE FOUNDATIONS OF THE INTERNATIONAL TRADE REGIME date back to 1947 when the General Agreement on Tariffs and Trade was concluded. This Agreement, salvaged from an unratified larger agreement called the International Trade Organization, was one piece of the so-called Bretton-Woods system, designed in the post-World War II environment to promote and manage global economic development. (The International Monetary Fund and International Bank for Reconstruction and Development—the World Bank—were the other two main pieces.) GATT established the two basic directions for the trade regime:

- Developing requirements to lower and eliminate tariffs, and

- Creating obligations to prevent or eliminate other types of impediments or barriers to trade (non-tariff barriers).

From 1948 to 1994, eight negotiating "Rounds" took place under the auspices of GATT to further develop the trade regime along both these lines. Early rounds focused more on tariffs alone, but non-tariff barriers have since come to the fore.

The last of these negotiations, the "Uruguay Round," concluded in 1994. The *Marrakech Agreement Establishing the World Trade Organization* marked the end of the Round. It also created the World Trade Organization. In this section, the basic elements of the WTO and its law are identified. These include the most important components, functions, principles and agreements that provide the foundation for today's modern trade regime.

3.1 Structure of the World Trade Organization

The World Trade Organization came into force on January 1, 1995, fully replacing the previous GATT Secretariat as the organization responsible for administering the international trade regime. The basic structure of the WTO includes the following bodies (see organizational diagram):

WTO structure

All WTO members may participate in all councils, committees, etc.,
except Appellate Body, Dispute Settlement panels, Textiles Monitoring Body, and plurilateral committees.

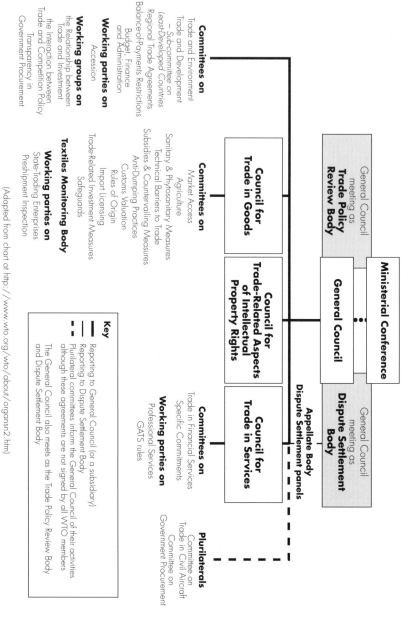

Ministerial Conference

General Council
meeting as
**Trade Policy
Review Body**

General Council

General Council
meeting as
**Dispute Settlement
Body**

**Appellate Body
Dispute Settlement panels**

**Council for
Trade in Goods**

**Council for
Trade-Related Aspects
of Intellectual
Property Rights**

**Council for
Trade in Services**

Committees on
Market Access
Agriculture
Sanitary & Phytosanitary Measures
Technical Barriers to Trade
Subsidies & Countervailing Measures
Anti-Dumping Practices
Customs Valuation
Rules of Origin
Import Licensing
Trade-Related Investment Measures
Safeguards

Textiles Monitoring Body

Working parties on
State-Trading Enterprises
Preshipment Inspection

Committees on
Trade in Financial Services
Specific Commitments

Working parties on
Professional Services
GATS rules

Plurilaterals
Committee on
Trade in Civil Aircraft
Committee on
Government Procurement

Committees on
Trade and Environment
Trade and Development
  – Sub-committee on
Least-Developed Countries
Regional Trade Agreements
Balance-of-Payments Restrictions
Budget, Finance
and Administration

Working parties on
Accession

Working groups on
the Relationship between
Trade and Investment
the Interaction between
Trade and Competition Policy
Transparency in
Government Procurement

Key
— Reporting to General Council (or a subsidiary)
- - Reporting to Dispute Settlement Body
Plurilateral committees inform the General Council of their activities
although these agreements are not signed by all WTO members
The General Council also meets as the Trade Policy Review Body
and Dispute Settlement Body

(Adapted from chart at http://www.wto.org/wto/about/organsn2.htm)

- *The Ministerial Conference*, which is composed of international trade ministers from all member countries. This is the governing body of the WTO, responsible for setting the strategic direction of the organization and making all final decisions on agreements under its wings. The Ministerial Conference meets at least once every two years. Although voting can take place, decisions are generally taken by consensus, a process that can at times be difficult, particularly in a body composed of 136 very different members.

- *The General Council*, composed of senior representatives (usually ambassador level) of all members. It is responsible for overseeing the day-to-day business and management of the WTO, and is based at the WTO headquarters in Geneva. In practice, this is the key decision-making arm of the WTO for most issues. Several of the bodies described below report directly to the General Council.

- *The Trade Policy Review Body* is also composed of all the WTO members, and oversees the Trade Policy Review Mechanism, a product of the Uruguay Round. It periodically reviews the trade policies and practices of all member states. These reviews are intended to provide a general indication of how states are implementing their obligations, and to contribute to improved adherence by the WTO parties to their obligations.

- *The Dispute Settlement Body* is also composed of all the WTO members. It oversees the implementation and effectiveness of the dispute resolution process for all WTO agreements, and the implementation of the decisions on WTO disputes. Disputes are heard and ruled on by dispute resolution panels chosen individually for each case, and the permanent Appellate Body that was established in 1994. Dispute resolution is mandatory and binding on all members. A final decision of the Appellate Body can only be reversed by a full consensus of the Dispute Settlement Body.

- *The Councils on Trade in Goods and Trade in Services* operate under the mandate of the General Council and are composed of all members. They provide a mechanism to oversee the details of the general and specific agreements on trade in goods (such as those on textiles and agriculture) and trade in services. There is also a Council for the Agreement on Trade-Related Aspects of Intellectual Property Rights, dealing with just that agreement and subject area.

- *The Secretariat and Director General* of the WTO reside in Geneva, in the old home of GATT. The Secretariat now numbers just under 550 people, and undertakes the administrative functions of running all aspects of the organization. The Secretariat has no legal decision-making powers but provides vital services, and often advice, to those who do. The Secretariat is headed by the Director General, who is elected by the members.

- ***The Committee on Trade and Development and Committee on Trade and Environment*** are two of the several committees continued or established under the *Marrakech Agreement* in 1994. They have specific mandates to focus on these relationships, which are especially relevant to how the WTO deals with sustainable development issues. The Committee on Trade and Development was established in 1965. The forerunner to the Committee on Trade and Environment (the Group on Environmental Measures and International Trade) was established in 1971, but did not meet until 1992. Both Committees are now active as discussion grounds but do not actually negotiate trade rules. The mandate of the CTE is discussed in greater detail in section 3.1.1.

3.1.1 The Committee on Trade and Environment

The terms of reference given to the CTE in Marrakech are, in part:

"To identify the relationship between trade measures and environmental measures, in order to promote sustainable development;

To make appropriate recommendations on whether any modifications of the provisions of the multilateral trading system are required, compatible with the open, equitable and non-discriminatory nature of the system..."

The Committee narrowed this broad mandate down to a 10-item agenda for work (see Box 3-1) and has used this agenda as its framework for discussions. Since 1996 the Committee has grouped the 10 items into two clusters for better focus: those items on the theme of market access (items 2, 3, 4 and 6), and those on the linkages between international environmental management and the trading system (items 1, 5, 7 and 8). Item 9, on trade in services, has not been much discussed, and item 10, on openness, sits in its own category.

Box 3-1: Work program of the Committee on Trade and Environment

The CTE has an agenda of 10 items for discussion:

1. The relationship between trade rules and trade measures used for environmental purposes, including those in MEAs.

2. The relationship between trade rules and environmental policies with trade impacts.

3. a) The relationship between trade rules and environmental charges and taxes.

   b) The relationship between trade rules and environmental requirements for products, including packaging, labelling and recycling standards and regulations.

4. Trade rules on the transparency (that is, full and timely disclosure) of trade measures used for environmental purposes, and of environmental policies with trade impacts.

5. The relationship between the dispute settlement mechanisms of the WTO and those of MEAs.

6. The potential for environmental measures to impede access to markets for developing country exports, and the potential environmental benefits of removing trade restrictions and distortions.

7. The issue of the export of domestically prohibited goods.

8. The relationship between the environment and the TRIPS Agreement.

9. The relationship between the environment and trade in services.

10. WTO's relations with other organizations, both non-governmental and inter-governmental.

3.2   Functions of the WTO

The main functions of the WTO can be described in very simple terms. These are:

- To oversee implementing and administering WTO agreements;

- To provide a forum for negotiations; and

- To provide a dispute settlement mechanism.

The goals behind these functions are set out in the preamble to the Marrakech Agreement. These include:

- Raising standards of living;

- Ensuring full employment;

- Ensuring large and steadily growing real incomes and demand; and

- Expanding the production of and trade in goods and services.

These objectives are to be achieved while allowing for the optimal use of the world's resources in accordance with the objective of sustainable development, and while seeking to protect and preserve the environment. The preamble also specifically mentions the need to assist developing countries, especially the least developed countries, secure a growing share of international trade.

3.3   The core principles

The WTO aims to achieve its objectives by reducing existing barriers to trade and by preventing new ones from developing. It seeks to ensure fair and equal competitive conditions for market access, and predictability of access for all traded goods and services. This approach is based on two fundamental principles: the national-treatment and most-favoured nation principles. Together, they form the critical "discipline" of *non-discrimination* at the core of trade law.

- The principle of national treatment requires, in its simplest terms, that the goods and services of other countries be treated in the same way as those of your own country.

- The most-favoured nation principle requires that if special treatment is given to the goods and services of one country, they must be given to all WTO member countries. No one country should receive favours that distort trade.

Members follow these principles of non-discrimination among "like products"—those of a similar quality that perform similar functions in a similar way. They are, of course, free to discriminate among products that are not like—foreign oranges need not be treated the same as domestic carrots. Note, however, that products that are not physically or chemically identical can still be considered like products if, among other things, the products have the same end use, perform to the same standards and require nothing different for handling or disposal. The "like products test," which tries to determine which products are and are not like, is thus of central importance. These two complementary principles and the notion of "like products" are discussed further in section 3.4.1.

Sustainable development: Some argue that the concept of sustainable development has now emerged as a principle to guide the interpretation of the WTO Agreements, though not at the level of the core principles of non-discrimination. In the 1998 Appellate Body ruling in the so-called shrimp-turtle case, it was made clear that the interpretation of WTO law should reflect the Uruguay Round's deliberate inclusion of the language and concept of sustainable development. This ruling may have moved the WTO toward requiring the legal provisions of its agreements to be interpreted and applied in light of the principles and legal standards of sustainable development.

How the WTO will use sustainable development as a principle of interpretation in the future remains, of course, to be seen. But it is clear that elevating "sustainable development" to this role would be a major step in making trade policy and sustainable development objectives mutually supporting.

3.4 The key agreements, with a special consideration of those related to the environment

Three key agreements under the WTO umbrella relate to environment and trade issues: the General Agreement on Tariffs and Trade; the Agreement on Technical Barriers to Trade; and the Agreement on Sanitary and Phytosanitary Measures. Many other agreements have environmental impacts and environmental provisions, and the issues they raise are discussed in greater detail in chapters 5 and 6. But the agreements and provisions discussed below have cross-cutting relevance to the environment-trade interface, and should be understood before the reader goes further.

3.4.1 The General Agreement on Tariffs and Trade, 1994

GATT is composed of 37 articles and a number of explanatory understandings and addenda. This section reviews a few selected articles that are of key environmental importance.

Articles I and III: Non-discrimination, like products

Articles I and III of GATT are the legal home of the core principles: most-favoured nation and national treatment. These principles were described earlier as together constituting the critical WTO discipline of non-discrimination.

Article I establishes the most-favoured nation rule. This requires parties to ensure that if special treatment is given to the goods or services of one country, they must be given to all WTO members. No one country should receive favours that distort trade. This provision originated because states had different tariff levels for different countries, and it was designed to reduce or eliminate those differences. The principle has now also been extended to other potential barriers to trade.

This rule has two major exceptions. The first applies to regional trade agreements. Where these have been adopted, preferential tariffs may be established between the parties to these agreements. The second exception is for developing countries, and especially the least developed countries. GATT allows members to apply preferential tariff rates, or zero tariff rates, to products coming from these countries while still having higher rates for like products from other countries. This exception is designed to help promote economic development where it is most needed.

Article III establishes the national-treatment rule. This requires that the products of other countries be treated the same way as like products manufactured in the importing country. No domestic laws should be applied to imported products to protect domestic producers from the competing (like) products. And imported products should receive treatment under national laws that "is no less favourable" than the treatment given to like domestic products.

Defining "like products" has important environmental implications. This issue will be explored further, when we discuss process and production methods in chapter 5, but for now it can be highlighted with an example. Consider two integrated circuit boards, one produced in a way that emits ozone-depleting substances, and another produced in a non-polluting way. Are these products like? If they are, then environmental regulators cannot give preference to the green product over the other when both arrive at the border. Nor can they discriminate against the polluting product if it arrives at the border to compete against domestically produced clean versions.

Although the term "like" has not been specifically defined, the WTO's dispute settlement system has several times had to wrestle with whether certain products were like, and has developed some criteria to help it do so. These include the end uses in a given market, consumer tastes and habits, and the products' properties, nature and qualities. Most recently, the dominant criterion that has emerged in applying the like-products test is commercial substitutability: do the two goods compete against each other in the market as substitutes? For example, although vodka and gin are not identical, their physical properties (alcohol content) and end use (drinking) are similar enough that they could be substituted one for the other. They might therefore be considered like.

Article XI: Quantitative restrictions and licences

Article XI of GATT imposes another type of limit on measures that a party can take to restrict trade. It prohibits the use of quotas, import or export licences, or similar measures related to the import or export of goods. This prohibition stems from the fact that such volume-based measures are more economically distorting than are price-based measures such as tariffs and taxes. Agricultural products currently benefit from an important exception to Article XI.

Article XI might conceivably lead to conflicts with the trade mechanisms in some MEAs. For example, the Basel Convention and CITES impose licence or permit requirements for trade in the materials they control. To date these types of provisions in MEAs have never been challenged under trade laws.

Article XX: The environmental exceptions

Normally, when a national law is inconsistent with trade rules the state must withdraw or modify the law within a reasonable time—usually within 15 to 18 months. Article XX of GATT, however, allows for certain specific exceptions to the rules. The two exceptions most relevant for environment-related measures are the following:

> *Subject to the requirement that such measures are not applied in a manner which would constitute a means of arbitrary or unjustifiable discrimination between countries where the same conditions prevail, or a disguised restriction on international trade, nothing in this Agreement shall be construed to prevent the adoption or enforcement by any contracting party of measures:...*
>
> *(b) necessary to protect human, animal or plant life or health;...*
>
> *(g) relating to the conservation of exhaustible natural resources if such measures are made effective in conjunction with restrictions on domestic production or consumption;*

A country wanting to use the environmental exceptions in Article XX has two hurdles to clear. It must first establish the *provisional justification* for using Article XX by showing that sub-paragraph (b) or (g) applies. It must then establish *final justification* by showing that the measure in question does not contravene the lead paragraph, or *chapeau*, quoted above.

Paragraph (b) requires the state to show that the measure is "necessary" to protect the environment. In the past, this test has required the state:

1. To demonstrate the necessity to protect its own environment;

2. To demonstrate the need to use a trade-impacting measure to do so; and

3. If a trade-impacting measure is needed, to ensure it is the least trade-restrictive measure available to achieve the objectives.

The second and third parts of the necessity test seek to reduce the potential trade impacts from environmental measures, and to prevent environmental measures from being used as a disguised restriction or disguised barrier to trade. The hurdle they create can be difficult to clear, particularly if the measure under dispute is measured against purely hypothetical alternatives, rather than alternatives that may actually be available and practical for environmental regulators. The first part of the test had been traditionally applied to rule out environmental laws that protected the environment outside the enacting country's borders, though the 1998 WTO Appellate Body ruling in the shrimp-turtle case may have changed this by requiring merely a "sufficient nexus" between the law and the environment of the enacting state. Although the ruling did not fully explore what constituted a sufficient nexus, it appears that transboundary impacts on air and water, or impacts on endangered and migratory species, for example, might provide such a nexus.

A state claiming an exception under paragraph (g) must demonstrate first that its law relates to the conservation of exhaustible natural resources. The shrimp-turtle case made progress, from an environmental perspective, in defining exhaustible natural resources broadly, to include living and non-living resources (including other species) and renewable and non-renewable resources. Second, the law must have been accompanied by domestic-level restrictions on management, production or consumption of the resource to be conserved. Finally, the law must be "primarily aimed at" the conservation objectives; it must show "a close relationship between means and ends."

Once a law passes the tests described above it must then pass the tests in the chapeau, or opening paragraph, of Article XX, which address *how* the law is applied. The three tests in the chapeau to be met are whether, in its application, the measure is arbitrarily discriminatory, unjustifiably discriminatory or constitutes a disguised restriction on trade. The clearest statement to date on these tests in an environmental context comes from the 1998 shrimp-turtle case. Although the Appellate Body did not try to define these terms, it arguably defined a number of criteria for *not* meeting the tests including, for example, the following:

- A state cannot require another state to adopt specific environmental technologies or measures—different technologies or measures that have the same final effect should be allowed.

- When applying a measure to other countries, regulating countries must take into account differences in the conditions prevailing in those other countries.

- Before enacting trade measures countries should attempt to enter into negotiations with the exporting state(s).

- Foreign countries affected by trade measures should be allowed time to make adjustments.

- Due process, transparency, appropriate appeals procedures and other procedural safeguards must be available to foreign states or producers to review the application of the measure.

3.4.2 The Agreement on Technical Barriers to Trade

The Agreement on Technical Barriers to Trade covers measures that might be non-tariff barriers to trade. These can include technical performance standards a product must meet to be imported or exported—for example, energy efficiency standards for washing machines. They may also include environmental, health, labour or other standards a product must meet during its lifecycle—for example, forest products must come from sustainably managed forests. The TBT Agreement dictates when such barriers may be allowed and what conditions must be met (notification, transparency in developing the rules, the use of international standards when appropriate, and so on). It applies fully to all government standards, including most levels of government. Non-governmental, non-mandatory standards are less strictly covered under what is called the Code of Good Practice. The differences in coverage are discussed in greater detail in the context of environmental standards and ecolabels, in section 5.4.

3.4.3 The Agreement on the Application of Sanitary and Phytosanitary Measures

The Agreement on Sanitary and Phytosanitary Standards deals with standards "necessary" to protect humans, animals and plants from certain hazards associated with the movement of plants, animals and foodstuffs in international trade. Most countries enact measures in these areas to protect the environment or human, animal and plant health from:

- The risks from pests, diseases and disease-related organisms entering the country with the traded goods; and

- The risks from chemicals, fertilizers, pesticides and herbicides, toxins, veterinary medicines in foods, beverages, or animal feed.

Like the TBT Agreement, the SPS Agreement provides the rules for when sanitary and phytosanitary measures may be allowed and what conditions they must meet (such as notification, transparency in developing the rules, the use of international standards when appropriate, and so on). It requires that standards be based on scientific evidence and that a risk assessment be undertaken. Special provision is made for temporary measures when current scientific information is insufficient to adopt permanent measures, making the SPS one of the few WTO Agreements to observe the principle of precaution.

3.5   Other agreements

Other agreements are relevant to longer-term relationships between the trade regime, environment and sustainable development, and are likely to be further negotiated in any future round. These include the Agreement on Agriculture, General Agreement on Trade in Services, Agreement on Government Procurement, the Agreement on Trade-Related Investment Measures and the working groups and possible negotiations on investment and competition policy.

3.6   Regional trade agreements

Although the WTO provides the central features of the global trade regime, there is also an increasing number of regional and bilateral free trade zones and agreements that build on the global commitments. In chapter 7, three of the most important and developed of these regional structures are described, particularly as they relate to environmental concerns: the North American Free Trade Agreement and its associated North American Agreement on Environmental Cooperation, the European Union, and the Mercosur group of South American countries.

3.7   Dispute settlement

The dispute settlement mechanism, with its ability to deliver binding decisions, is one of the central elements of the Uruguay Round Agreements. The Dispute Settlement Understanding introduced a more structured dispute settlement process with more clearly defined stages than that which existed under GATT since 1947. A fundamental difference between the two is that under GATT a positive consensus was needed to adopt reports, so any one party could prevent formally adopting a decision. Under the DSU, dispute settlement reports are automatically adopted, unless consensus is to the contrary. This is known as "reverse consensus" and makes the decisions very difficult to reject. The DSU did, however, add a mechanism for appealing rulings to an Appellate Body.

A dispute is brought to the WTO when a member state believes that a fellow member is violating trade rules. This usually occurs when a company brings the violation to the attention of its government. The two parties to a dispute then follow a pre-defined set of procedures (see Box 3-2).

Box 3-2: Four phases of the dispute settlement mechanism

Consultations: Parties to a dispute are obliged to see if they can settle their differences. If consultations are not successful within 60 days, the complainant can ask the Dispute Settlement Body to establish a panel. The parties may also undertake good offices, conciliation, or mediation procedures.

The Panel: The three-member panel decides the case in a quasi-judicial process. Where the dispute involves a developing country, one panellist is from a developing country. The panel report, circulated to all WTO members within nine months of panel establishment, becomes the ruling of the DSB unless it is rejected by consensus or appealed.

Appeals: The possibility of appealing a panel ruling is a new feature in the DSM as compared with GATT. Either party can appeal the ruling of the panel based on points of law. Appeals are heard by three randomly selected members of the Appellate Body and may uphold, modify or reverse the legal findings and conclusions of the panel in a report issued within 60 to 90 days.

Surveillance of implementation: The violating member is required to state its intentions on implementation within 30 days of the report being adopted by the DSB. If the party fails to implement the report within a reasonable period (usually between eight and 15 months), the two countries enter negotiations to agree on appropriate compensation. If this fails, the prevailing party may ask the DSB for permission to retaliate, by imposing, for example, trade sanctions, the level of which is subject to arbitration.

The DSM cannot force a state to change its laws, even if they are found to contravene WTO rules. States intent on keeping such laws can either negotiate compensation for the complainant (for example, increasing the access to markets in another area), or failing that, be subjected to retaliatory trade sanctions. The EU–U.S. beef hormones case offers an example of this dynamic at work.

Suggested readings

Structure and functions of the WTO

About the WTO. WTO. <http://www.wto.org/wto/about/about.htm>.

IISD. *The WTO and sustainable development: An independent assessment.* Winnipeg: IISD, 1996. <http://iisd.ca/trade/wto/wtoreport.htm>.

Jackson, John. *The world trading system: Law and policy of the world trading system.* Cambridge: MIT Press, 1989.

The key agreements

South Centre. *The WTO multilateral trade agenda and the South.* Geneva: South Centre, 1998.
<http://www.southcentre.org/publications/wto/multilateral_.pdf>.

WTO legal texts. WTO. <http://www.wto.org/wto/legal/legal.htm>.

Dispute settlement

WTO dispute settlement. WTO. <http://www.wto.org/wto/dispute/dispute.htm>.

WWF International, Centre for International Environmental Law, Community Nutrition Institute and Oxfam. *Dispute settlement in the WTO: a crisis for sustainable development.* Gland: WWF International, 1998. <http://www.panda.org/resources/publications/sustainability/wto-98/fifth.htm>.

–4–
Physical and economic linkages

IN THE INTRODUCTION we argued that there is no simple pattern to the relationship between trade, environment and development. Depending on the sector, the country, the markets and prevailing policies, trade and trade liberalization may be good or bad for the environment and development. In fact, they will usually be both at once—good in some ways, bad in others.

This chapter illustrates the point by listing and explaining the complex physical and economic linkages that bind trade and sustainable development. For the most part, these consist of the impacts of trade on environment and development. The next chapter, on legal and regulatory linkages, widens the scope to also include the impacts of environmental concerns and environmental law on trade.

Trade flows and trade liberalization have at least four types of physical and economic impacts on environment and development: product effects, technology effects, scale effects and structural effects.[1] Each of these is examined in turn below.

4.1 Product effects

Product effects occur when the traded products themselves have an impact on the environment or development. On the *positive* side, trade may lead to spreading of new technologies for protecting the environment, such as microbial techniques for cleaning up oil spills. Or it may more rapidly spread goods or technologies that have less environmental impact—for example, solar power technology or more fuel-efficient automobiles—than those currently used. Openness to trade and investment can also help contribute to development objectives, by facilitating transfer of new and improved technologies and management systems.

On the *negative* side trade can facilitate international movement of goods that, from an environmental perspective, would best never be traded. With hazardous

---

1 This taxonomy is based on the work of the OECD. See *The environmental effects of trade*, Paris: OECD, 1994.

wastes and toxic materials, the environmental risks increase the further the goods are transported, since spillage is always possible. As well, such "goods" may end up being dumped in countries without the technical or administrative capacity to properly dispose of them, or even assess whether they should be accepted. Trade also makes possible the over-exploitation of species to the point of extinction—there is rarely enough domestic demand to create such pressure. The Basel Convention and CITES, discussed earlier, are MEAs that restrict such trade because of its negative direct effects.

A subset of product effects, sometimes termed "technology effects," are associated with changes in the way products are made depending on the technology used. Technology effects stem from the way in which trade liberalization affects technology transfer and the production processes used to make traded goods. Positive technology effects result when the output of pollution per unit of economic product is reduced. Foreign producers may transfer cleaner technologies abroad when a trade measure or agreement results in a more open market and a business climate more conducive to investment. Trade-induced growth and competitive market pressures generated by liberalization can hasten processes of capital and technological modernization for all firms. Newly opened markets can provide the revenue and the income to allow firms to accelerate capital turnover, and invest in cleaner, more efficient plants, technologies and processes.

On the other hand trade liberalization and an expanded marketplace may harm more environmentally friendly and socially valuable traditional production methods. Trade liberalization can also promote the spread and use of harmful, less-environmentally friendly technologies. Whether technology effects stemming from liberalization have an overall positive or negative effect on the environment will depend considerably on other conditions and policies in the marketplace that determine availability and choice of those technologies (for example, price and national environmental regulation). These effects are reflected again under the heading "imported efficiency" in Box 4-1.

4.2   Scale effects

Trade and trade liberalization can expand the level of economic activity possible by making that activity more efficient. Box 4-1 explains the ways in which trade can increase efficiency, producing more goods with the same given set of natural resources, labour, machines and technology.

This expansion—essentially creating additional wealth—can have *positive* effects on the environment and development. It has obvious development benefits; although development is more than economic growth, such growth is essential for development in most Southern countries. We should note, however, three important qualifications to this positive link between trade and development:

- First, distributional considerations matter. That is, if trade increases inequity by creating wealth that is mostly concentrated in the hands of the wealthy, then it works against important development objectives.

- Second, not everyone will benefit from trade liberalization; inherent in the wealth-creating process is destruction of inefficient firms and sectors.

- Third, the potential of trade to increase wealth is just that: potential. To enjoy trade's full potential countries may need to devote, for example, a large amount of resources to building capacity in their export sectors.

Where trade creates wealth two types of environmental benefits may follow. First, increased efficiency can directly benefit the environment, since efficient firms need fewer natural resource inputs and produce less polluting waste. In this sense, the basis of comparative advantage—efficient use of resources—also underlies the goal of sustainable development.

Second, efficiency can benefit the environment indirectly by making people wealthier, and thus more likely to demand stronger environmental protection. This is not to say that the poor do not value the environment; indeed, their poverty may mean they depend on it more directly than do the rich. But it may be a lower priority than it would for those with stable employment and adequate income, food and housing. Much evidence suggests that richer economies will likely have lower levels of some harmful emissions than poorer ones (though this relationship does not hold for pollution and environmental degradation whose effects are felt far away in time or in space, such as greenhouse gas emissions). Where trade alleviates extreme poverty, it may save people from a vicious cycle whereby they are forced to degrade their environment to survive, in the process becoming increasingly impoverished.

Box 4-1. Improving efficiency: How trade can create wealth

Allocative efficiency. Liberalizing trade allows countries to specialize in producing those items at which they are relatively more efficient—at which they have a "comparative advantage." This allows more goods and services to be produced by nations that engage in trade, and so increases GDP. The other side of this coin is that trade restrictions or distortions tend to decrease allocative efficiency. For example, if a Northern country put enough tariff protection or subsidies in place, and devoted enough greenhouses and energy, it could produce coffee for its own market. But this would be economically inefficient and environmentally damaging.

Efficiency from competition. Another way in which trade creates wealth is to expose domestic firms to foreign competition, and thereby force them to innovate to become more efficient. Sometimes, better provision of goods can directly serve development objectives, as in the case of telecommunications and other such infrastructure provision. Again, these efficiency benefits are missed where trade is restricted or distorted. Of course, even efficient domestic producers may suffer if exposed to competition from firms with international monopoly power.

Imported efficiency. A third way in which trade can create wealth is through openness to foreign investment, or imports of foreign technology, which can bring more efficient methods of process and production. These can be embodied in a piece of equipment, or in the management techniques brought by a foreign firm setting up shop in a host country. Some multinational firms adhere to a global standard, and bring the same level of technology and practice to all their locations worldwide. Others will diminish the imported efficiency effect by using outdated, less efficient technology in countries where health, safety and environmental protection is more lax.

An increased scale of economic activity can also have *negative* environmental effects. Most economic activity damages the environment, whether in extracting raw materials, harvesting renewable resources, or in creating waste and pollution. Increasing the scale of economic activity means increasing the levels of environmental damage, unless regulations are in place to ensure that the additional activities cause no harm—an unlikely scenario.

Another possible negative effect stems from the additional wealth created by trade—the same wealth that, as noted above, can benefit the environment and development. For some types of pollution, increased wealth may mean more, not less pollution. The richer countries of the world, for example, have far higher per capita emissions of all types of greenhouse gases than do developing countries, and far higher per capita emissions of such toxins as PCBs, dioxins and furans. With enough wealth comes the opportunity to consume at levels and in ways that are worse for the environment.

4.3 Structural effects

Trade liberalization will lead to changes in the composition of a country's economy, causing it to produce more of the goods it makes well or has in abundance, to trade for those it does not. For example, a heavily forested country that did not trade would produce only enough forest products for its own people. Under a trading scenario it might produce enough for export as well, increasing the size of forestry's slice in the nation's economic pie. This kind of structural effect can be either positive or negative for the environment and development.

On the *positive* side, if the composition of the economy changes so that less polluting sectors have a bigger share of the pie, then trade has resulted in environmental improvements (at least at the national level; the polluting firms may have simply moved to a different country). Similarly, trade liberalization would help foster development if the composition of the economy changed to include sectors or firms with stronger links to the domestic economy, increased employment prospects, or otherwise enhanced potential for creating income equity.

Trading with a country whose consumers demand green goods may also change the composition of the economy, if exporters respond by creating new products or sectors. A number of coffee producers in Mexico, for example, have collaborated on marketing organically grown coffee, which can be sold at premium prices. The potential environmental benefits are obvious. Usually the impetus for a green shift in composition comes not from final buyers of goods, but from other firms buying inputs. For example, Ford and GM, two giants of U.S. automobile manufacturing, have declared that they will soon buy only from suppliers that are certified as following the ISO 14001 environmental management system. If ISO certification leads to environmental improvements, then Ford and GM will have forced such improvements down the supply chain to foreign and domestic suppliers.

Also on the positive side, trade liberalization may remove subsidies, quotas or other trade-restrictive measures that frustrate allocative efficiency. To use the fictitious example cited in Box 4-1, if trade liberalization forced a Northern country to stop protecting its own coffee industry, the resources that had been used for that industry could go to other more productive uses. This would have significant development benefits for the countries where coffee grows naturally, which could increase their exports. It would also have environmental benefits. For example, far less heat (or none) from fossil fuels would be needed to grow the same value of more traditional produce in the former coffee greenhouses.

On the *negative* side, if the goods that a country makes well are based on natural resources, or are pollution-intensive, then trade liberalization would increase the share of such industries in the national economy. Without appropriate environmental policies this would mean increased pollution, or accelerated harvesting of natural resources such as fish or timber, perhaps at unsustainable levels. When liberalization creates opportunities for this type of trade, linking domestic natural resources to international demand, environmental degradation and resource depletion can be rapid. Adding to these direct effects, the resulting scale of activity can overwhelm existing domestic structures for regulation. Similarly, trade liberalization may change the mix of industries to attract those that do little to help advance development objectives.

Another set of possible negative effects of economic openness is related to timing of liberalization, and the transitional process of economic restructuring. These result from openness not only to trade in goods and services, but also to flows of investment (for example, direct investment, portfolio investment and currency speculation). More and more research shows that timing is crucial in liberalizing regimes for trade and investment. Small developing economies in particular may be hamstrung by geographical, sectoral or institutional problems that cannot be quickly overcome. In the meantime, liberalization may produce a painful and protracted transition. In these economies, experience has shown that economic openness must be properly staged, and accompanied by policies specifically designed to ease the restructuring process. Otherwise, liberalization may, at least in the short and medium term, actually work against growth, employment, poverty alleviation, environmental protection and other components of sustainable development.

Suggested readings

Anderson, K. and R. Blackhurst, eds. *The greening of world trade issues.* New York: Harvester Wheatsheaf and The University of Michigan Press, 1992.

Nordstrom, Hakan and Scott Vaughan. *Trade and environment* (special studies #4). Geneva: WTO, 1999.

OECD. *The environmental effects of trade.* Paris: OECD, 1994.

–5–
Legal and policy linkages

THE PREVIOUS SECTION DESCRIBED the ways in which trade, environment and development were related at a physical and economic level, mostly focusing on the impacts of trade on environment and development. This section looks at a different class of linkages—the interactions between trade law and environmental law. It was noted earlier that environmental law increasingly dictates how countries shall structure their economies (for example the Kyoto Protocol will, if successful, involve massive changes in investment and production decisions), and trade law increasingly defines how countries should structure their domestic laws and policies in areas such as environmental protection. It is inevitable, then, that the two systems of law and policy will interact.

These can occur at two levels—the national or the international. Nationally, the areas of policy we will treat include subsidies, environmental labelling, intellectual property rights, agriculture, investment, and government procurement. We will also look at national-level environmental standards as they relate to three subjects: discrimination based on the use of process and production methods, the competitiveness effects of different levels of standards between countries, and policy-making under uncertainty. Internationally, we will look at the interaction of the multilateral system of trade with the multilateral regimes for environmental management.

5.1 Environmental standards and process and production methods

"PPM" has become one of the most debated sets of letters in trade law history. For many people, this debate lies at the heart of the trade and environment relationship.

A process and production method is the way in which a product is made. Many products go through a number of stages, and therefore a number of PPMs, before they are ready for market. For example, making paper requires trees to be grown and harvested, the wood to be processed, the pulp often to be bleached, and so on. The various processes will have different sorts of envi-

41

ronmental impacts—on biodiversity, on forest-based streams and wildlife, on human health from chemical pollution of waterways, or in terms of air pollution and energy use. Other paper may be made from post-consumer waste, a different process involving a different set of environmental impacts.

An important technical distinction is the difference between a product-related PPM and a non-product related PPM (see Box 5-1). Throughout this book the term PPMs will refer to non-product-related PPMs, more or less the accepted shorthand in general discourse.

Box 5-1: Product- and non-product-related PPMs

The distinction between product-related PPMs and non-product-related PPMs may seem like nitpicking, but it is important to understand, since the two are treated entirely differently under trade law.

The distinction rests on how the PPM affects the final product. Consider two products—say two rolls of newsprint. One is produced using 50 per cent recycled content, and the other is produced from 100 per cent virgin fibre. These are two very different PPMs. But the key question is whether the final product has different qualities that would cause it to be treated differently in its use, handling or disposal. If the recycled newsprint performs in every sense the same as the virgin-content product, then the recycled-content process is a *non-product related PPM*, since it has a negligible impact on the final product.

Take, for another example, two apples—one produced organically and one produced with the use of pesticides, some of which are still left on the product as a residue. Again we have two very different PPMs. But in this case, the difference will cause us to have to handle and use (but probably not dispose of) the products differently. Some people might want to peel the chemically treated apple, and border authorities will inspect the levels of pesticide residue to see that they meet health regulations. The organic apple may be subject to tighter border checks aimed at preventing the spread of invasive pests. The different PPMs in this case make a difference to the final product, and they would thus treated as *product-related* PPMs.

Trade law does not question the right of countries to discriminate based on product-related PPMs. There are rules about the *process* of discrimination, of course—the SPS Agreement, for example, has a preference for international standards when setting restrictions on pesticide residue levels—but the *prin-*

ciple of discrimination is accepted. Non-product-related PPMs, on the other hand, make no difference to the commercial or practical substitutability of the products—a criterion that we noted in chapter 3 is increasingly being used in the WTO to determine which products are like. And, we noted, WTO law does not allow countries to discriminate among like products, whatever their different environmental impacts.

This prohibition makes little environmental sense. The way a product is produced is one of the three central questions for an environmental manager: how is it made, how is it used and how is it disposed of. Domestic environmental regulations on PPMs abound—factories are told how much pollution they may emit, forest products companies are told how and where they may harvest trees, mining companies are told how they must treat their waste, and how they must restore their sites after mine closure. So from an environmental perspective, it makes sense to also be able to discriminate at the border between otherwise like goods that were produced in clean and dirty ways.

In practice, however, allowing discrimination based on PPMs would present some difficulties for the trading system. It would give governments greater opportunity in their struggle to protect their industries unfairly against foreign competition. Motivated not by environmental but by economic considerations, a government might conduct an inventory of the environmentally preferable PPMs used by its domestic industries, and make new regulations penalizing those producers (that is, foreigners) not using them.

At least this might result in environmental improvement, if only in certain selected industries, and only if the inefficiencies thus created did not overwhelm the environmental benefits. (See the discussion in chapter 2 of efficiency and the environment.) But there are two other fears. The first is that the standards thus imposed might be environmentally inappropriate for some foreign competitors. For example, a country where water scarcity is a major issue might enact laws discriminating against products produced in ways that waste water. But this would force exporters in water-rich countries to follow standards that are not relevant to their local environmental conditions.

The second is a related argument from some developing countries that argue that their social priorities differ from those of developed countries. They may, for example, be more concerned about clean water as an environmental issue than with global warming. Or they may be more concerned about infrastructure, education and health care than about *any* environmental issue. If so, the argument goes, it is unfair for developed countries to discriminate against their exports based on environmental issues that are not high on their agendas, forcing them to either adopt rich country environmental priorities or suffer a loss of wealth-creating exports. Many developing countries worry that if the WTO allows PPM-based discrimination on environmental grounds, it will also be forced to allow it on social grounds, such as human rights, labour standards and so on, increasing the scope of the threat to their exports.

Another part of this argument is that the now-rich countries became wealthy by burning a lot of fossil fuels, cutting down most of their forests, destroying the ozone layer and otherwise cashing in on national and global environmental resources. Now that the wealth they have gained allows them to maintain high environmental standards, it is hypocritical to forbid developing countries to follow the same path. At a minimum such demands should be accompanied by technical and financial assistance to help bring about environmental improvements, and other forms of capacity building.

Finally, there is a sovereignty argument. If the environmental damage in question is purely local, then it is really the purview of the exporting, not the importing, government. This argument weakens, however, if the environmental damage in question is not purely local—if it involves polluting shared waters or airstreams, depleting populations of species that migrate across borders, or damaging the atmosphere. Here, the need for international co-operation is obvious.

MEAs are one such form of co-operation, and are the most commonly recommended way to prevent PPM-based environment and trade conflicts. That is, countries should collectively agree to either harmonize standards or to live with a negotiated menu of different national standards. As we have seen, many such agreements are in force today. Such agreements, however, take many years to negotiate and even more to take full affect—a problem, if the environmental issue in question is urgent. As well, some subject areas may not be ripe for agreement; countries often disagree on the need to regulate or the mechanisms for doing so. These factors may make the international option unattractive for addressing issues of great importance to some countries.

5.2 Environmental standards and competitiveness

In developed countries a key concern of the environmental community is the prospect of a "race to the bottom," where countries try to lure investment by lowering or not enforcing their environmental standards. This is the "pollution haven" argument—that under free trade firms will migrate to places where environmental regulations are less stringent and where using "dirty" PPMs will give them a competitive edge.

Researchers have long searched for evidence of pollution havens, and have found little. When relocating, environmental costs are only one of a broad number of factors—including infrastructure, access to inputs, wage costs, labour productivity and political risk—a firm must take into account. Average environmental control costs run around 2 to 3 per cent of total costs, though in certain sectors (for example, aluminum smelting or cement manufacturing) it can run much higher.

The *threat* of relocation by firms may be more of an issue than actual relocation. The threat, whether made explicitly or just anticipated, may create a "regulatory chill" effect—a climate where government regulators balk at strengthening their environmental laws for fear of driving away existing business, or losing potential business investment.

The same types of concerns about competitiveness underlie the problems that many commodities exporters face in trying to implement appropriate environmental policies. Such policies would help internalize the external environmental costs of production, and would therefore often raise the price of the final good. For most commodities even a slight rise in price may be enough to send buyers to one of the many competitors. And commodities, unlike consumer goods or manufactures, usually cannot create niche markets for greener goods. Buyers of copper, for example, want the cheapest copper that meets their technical specifications, and they typically do not care about the pollution created in its manufacture. This is a serious problem, given the importance of commodity exports to many developing nation economies, and the wide-ranging environmental consequences of most commodity production.

5.3   Environmental standards, science and precaution

Science is the starting point of all environmental policy. Without science we have no way of knowing what is happening in the natural environment, beyond what our senses tell us. Science makes the environment speak, and all policy-making is based on interests that have voices. But the scientific method does not always generate precise information for policy-making—scientific knowledge is rarely either certain or complete. And even where science is quite certain—for example, in its assertion that certain gases in the atmosphere trap heat and can change the planet's climate—the implications for policy can be obscure.

The tension between science and policy is a constant theme of international environmental regimes. All of these regimes have some method of reviewing new scientific evidence, often through their Conference of Parties, sometimes through their own subsidiary bodies, or, in exceptional cases such as the climate regime, through specially created independent organizations such as the Intergovernmental Panel on Climate Change.

The precautionary principle, described in chapter 2 as a basic environmental principle, counsels that environmental measures must sometimes be adopted even when scientific information is incomplete. It has proven difficult to implement since it requires that policy-makers exercise some discretion. For this reason it is important to develop criteria governing its application. Among other things, these criteria would address a balance of two important considerations: the scale of possible damage, and the cost of action—or of inaction.

As the scale of possible damage increases, so does the need to act with precaution. Where the potential damage is obvious, as with stratospheric ozone depletion, the need for action becomes clearer and less contentious. Where the potential is less obvious, precautionary action can become extremely contentious, as affected stakeholders seek to protect their interests. Indeed, it is normal to expect controversy over action on such issues as genetically modified organisms, where the science is still unclear and is evolving rapidly.

Some governments use the tools of risk assessment to minimize the scope for discretion in applying the precautionary principle. This will delay action, and can leave so many issues unresolved that decision-making is not necessarily facilitated.

Cost is the other criterion to consider in applying the precautionary principle. Resources are limited so governments must make tough decisions about where to apply them. Clearly, precautionary actions that are without net economic cost should be taken. But since such actions may involve losses in one area, even though they are counterbalanced by gains in another, they may still attract vigorous opposition from the losers. *Inaction* may also incur costs—the costs of environmental damage unchecked—and these can be enormous. It is important that these be part of the calculations, where they will weigh against the costs of action.

5.4   Ecolabelling and environmental management system certification programs

Environmental labels (or ecolabels) and environmental management system certification programs, like MEAs, are touted as a possible solution to the problems with PPMs mentioned earlier. That is, rather than governments dictating by law which PPMs are acceptable, consumers can decide for themselves, informed by labels and certifications, and purchase accordingly. Unlike government laws and regulations, these are voluntary tools, providing information that helps consumers make informed choices. Ecolabels inform consumers about a specific product, whereas EMS certification schemes tell them something about the companies (or parts thereof) that produce the products. This section first defines the two instruments, and then looks at how they might interact with the rules of international trade.

5.4.1 Ecolabels

Ecolabels tell us about the environmental impacts from producing or using a product. They are voluntary, but in some markets they are becoming an important competitive factor. There are many different labelling programs, run by governments, private companies and non-governmental organizations, but all boil down to three basic types of label (see Box 5-2). The Geneva-based International Organization for Standardization is establishing standards for each.

Box 5-2: Ecolabels according to the ISO—the three types

Type I labels compare products with others within the same category, awarding labels to those that are environmentally preferable through their whole life cycle. The criteria are set by an independent body and monitored through a certification, or auditing, process. Ranking products in this way requires tough judgement calls: consider two otherwise identical products, one air polluting, another water polluting. Which is superior?

Type II labels are environmental claims made about goods by their manufacturers, importers or distributors. They are not independently verified, do not use pre-determined and accepted criteria for reference, and are arguably the least informative of the three types of environmental labels. A label claiming a product to be "biodegradable," without defining the term, is a type II label.

Type III labels list a menu of a product's environmental impacts throughout its life cycle. They are similar to nutrition labels on food products that detail fat, sugar or vitamin contents. The information categories can be set by industrial sector or by independent bodies. Unlike type I labels, they do not judge products, leaving that task to consumers. Critics question whether the average consumer has the time and knowledge to judge whether, for example, emissions of sulphur are more threatening than emissions of cadmium.

5.4.2 Environmental management system certification

EMS certification schemes assess a company's overall handling of environmental issues. Unlike ecolabels, these schemes do not imply anything about the environmental impacts of companies' products. Rather, they require companies to follow preset environmental principles and guidelines they set themselves as they conduct business. The requirements in such voluntary schemes are often flexible and open to interpretation, and are generally less contentious than ecolabelling schemes.

The ISO 14001 environmental management system standard is one such scheme at the international level. ISO 14001 helps companies track, understand and improve their environmental management. Unlike sector-specific certifications, ISO 14001 does not require specific principles or guidelines to be followed. Companies can "self-certify" compliance with the standard, but most seek independent verification. Critics maintain that ISO 14001 says nothing about a company's environmental performance, addressing only the effectiveness of its environmental management system. ISO 14001 can be useful, however, in that it forces companies to acknowledge and address environmental issues.

Somewhere between an ecolabel and an EMS certification is a new class of sector-specific environmental certifications, such as those that have been developed for the forestry, fisheries, organic agriculture, and tourism sectors. A company obtains certification if an independent auditor finds that it satisfies principles and criteria set out in the scheme. An industry focus allows the scheme's guidance to be more specific than a generic system like ISO 14001. Certification typically allows the company to place what amounts to an ecolabel on its product, certifying compliance.

5.4.3 Ecolabels, EMS certification and international trade

As consumers become more aware of environmental issues, the demand for green goods and companies grows. Ecolabels and EMS certification programs help by giving consumers the information they need to make environmentally sound purchasing decisions. But they may also create problems, both of principle and of process, at the international level.

The problem of principle is the same as that described earlier for PPMs and applies mostly to ecolabels, since they are often a means for consumers to practice PPM-based discrimination. Most ecolabelling schemes are national programs, developed for domestic economic and environmental realities, and consider domestic environmental preferences. The criteria developed by this process may be irrelevant to the environmental and social priorities of other countries. For example, forest conservation is a priority for some countries—particularly those where regrowth is slow—and consumers may therefore want an ecolabel to be awarded for the recycled content in paper. But this will disqualify paper from other countries where the climate allows for profitable sustainably managed forest plantations, whose product content is 100 per cent virgin pulp.

The problem of process relates to the procedures that foreign producers must follow to get awarded an ecolabel or a certification. Testing procedures may require technologies, infrastructure and expertise that are not available in some countries, particularly in the South. Even if such testing can be done, it will involve much higher costs than those incurred by Northern producers. For example, the technology needed to test for genetically modified organisms in food products is very expensive. The market opportunities offered by an eco-label that notes a product is GMO free might therefore be more limited in countries without existing testing facilities and in those that depend on low labour and capital costs.

Another process concern relates to setting international standards for certifi-cation and developing ecolabels by bodies such as the ISO. Although these efforts are acknowledged as helping make the processes more open, and as fos-tering mutual recognition of claims among countries, they are also extremely expensive and time-consuming for those delegates involved. This leads to few developing countries being represented. As well, the process frequently lacks transparency. As a result, some fear that international standardizing bodies may be just more fora where Western countries will act strategically to protect their dominant market positions.

5.5   Subsidies

Subsidies are one of the clearest areas of shared interest for the trade and envi-ronment communities. Both oppose so-called perverse subsidies—subsidies that are harmful to the environment and the economy. And there may also be scope for co-operation on allowing new subsidies that benefit the environment without unduly distorting trade.

Depending on the definition, perverse subsidies worldwide range from $500 billion to $1.5 trillion a year. This is a powerful force for environmental dam-age and economic inefficiency. At the environment-trade nexus, a number of sectors are of interest, with agriculture, forestry, energy, transportation and fisheries being the most obvious.

Environmentalists and advocates of free trade dislike perverse subsidies because they distort prices. From an environmental perspective, they artifi-cially lower the costs of doing business in an environmentally unsustainable way. Subsidies in the fisheries sector, for example, include low-interest loans to fishermen, fuel tax exemptions, and outright grants to purchase gear, boats and other infrastructure. These measures all lower the cost of fishing and lead to overexploitation of the resource—too many fishermen and too many boats chasing too few fish. In other sectors the story follows the same basic plot. Agriculture, energy production and transportation are all hard on the envi-ronment, and most of the environmental damage they entail is not built into the market price of the goods they produce. The consumer buying bread, for example, is not paying for any of the environmental costs incurred in growing the wheat. Subsidizing wheat growers may therefore increase environmental damage, by increasing their scale of operations. To add insult to injury, subsidizing polluting sectors or technologies reduces incentives to develop greener alternatives. The $145 billion a year given in subsidies to the fossil fuel and nuclear energy sectors worldwide diverts physical, financial and intellectual capital from research and development for alternatives like solar energy.

From an economic perspective, distorted prices reduce one of the main potential gains from trade—increased efficiency (see chapter 4). If Iceland, for example, devoted enough subsidies to the production of coffee in greenhouses it could become a competitive exporter. But most people would agree that this would be a staggering waste of resources for the Icelandic economy.

It is important to remember that not all subsidies are perverse. A subsidy that pays for previously unpaid environmental benefits may be socially desirable. For example, it may make sense for governments to subsidize developing and disseminating solar technologies as alternatives to fossil fuels since it could lower emissions of greenhouse gases. If environmental costs are factored in, such subsidies actually move prices closer to their true level. The WTO recognizes that some sorts of subsidies are desirable, and has provided an exception in the Agreement on Subsidies and Countervailing Measures that allows for certain subsidies to firms to meet new environmental regulations (up to 20 per cent of the costs of a one-time expenditure). As well, a number of proposals for WTO rules have been made to allow subsidies to encourage the spread of environmentally sound technologies.

Even those subsidies that are perverse deserve careful analysis. Dismantling them can cause hardship in the short run to those least able to absorb the shock. Cutting fossil fuel subsidies in cold climates, for example, may hurt the poor who depend on such subsidies to heat their homes. Cutting fisheries subsidies may mean an initial loss of needed revenue for countries that sell the rights to fish their territorial waters. These types of considerations argue for bridging measures to accompany subsidy removal.

It remains to be seen whether the WTO can play a major role in dismantling perverse subsidies. A number of proposals have been put forward to have the WTO help reduce perverse fisheries subsidies, and the question of how to design appropriate agricultural subsidies is being informed by environmental concerns (see section 5.6). But building consensus on such changes will not be an easy task—for every perverse subsidy there is a host of beneficiaries keen to see things stay as they are.

5.6   Agriculture

Changes in the laws that govern international agricultural trade will have major and complex sustainable development impacts. Agriculture and trade in agriculture are economically important for virtually all regions of the world. The highly industrialized economies are overwhelmingly dominant as both exporters and importers of agricultural products, with the U.S. clearly in a leader's position. But the relative importance of agricultural trade to economies in Asia, Latin America and Africa is rising.

Agriculture is also of key environmental importance. Irrigation is the largest single user of water in most countries. Agricultural runoff and seepage of fertilizers and pesticides are major sources of groundwater pollution. Changing patterns of land use, for example from forest to agriculture, can destroy habitat for plant and animal species. Intensive livestock operations in many countries have grown so large that they pose major problems of waste management and disposal, and are sources of air and water pollution.

Changing patterns of trade and production can have social as well as environmental impacts. Falling prices can increase pressures to migrate from farms, affecting the health of rural communities and institutions as well as reducing the human and financial capital available for long-term maintenance of the land.

Agriculture was arguably the subject of the most difficult negotiations of the Uruguay Round. Previously, agriculture had been accorded special status that allowed countries to protect their domestic industries in ways not permitted in other sectors. The Uruguay Round's Agreement on Agriculture was a first step to bringing agriculture under the normal rule of trade law, mandating among other things the capping of farm export subsidies, reductions in both the value of subsidies and the volume of subsidized exports, and reductions in the domestic support provided to farmers. Part of the Uruguay Round's built-in agenda—the ongoing schedule of work mandated in the Agreements—is a review of the Agreement on Agriculture, which began in 1999. Some of the issues this review may address are discussed below.

From an environmental perspective, one of the key areas of interest in the liberalization agenda is subsidies and other forms of support. At the outset, it is important to distinguish between support that distorts production decisions, and support that does not affect production. A subsidy paid for each hectare under cultivation, for example, affects production by encouraging more land to be cultivated. Farm income insurance, on the other hand, is a form of support that has no such undesirable incentives (though some economists argue that *any* payment to farmers distorts production decisions—even income insurance reduces risks and thus increases expected returns). This type of nondistorting support is termed "decoupled," and is preferred by both economists and environmentalists.

What is wrong with production-linked support? Simply, such support encourages too much production. This intensifies all the environmental problems discussed above. Sometimes it also leads to abandoning traditional sustainable practices such as rotating crops and fallowing fields. The incentives are huge: Western industrialized countries in 1996 poured an estimated $302 billion in support (not all of it production-linked) into the agricultural sector. Other forms of agricultural subsidies artificially lower the prices of inputs, such as water, fertilizers and pesticides, encouraging their overuse.

Agricultural support is also a key development issue. Many developing countries have an advantage in agricultural products compared with their developed country trading partners, but are unable to harness this potential engine for growth. Subsidized exports of surpluses from developed countries depress prices on the international markets, making agriculture a less profitable proposition for those whose governments cannot afford to subsidize.

The commitments made in the Uruguay Round begin to address some of these problems. Developed countries were given six years to cut their average agricultural tariffs by 36 per cent, to reduce their aggregate measures of support by 20 per cent and to cut export subsidies by 36 per cent. Developing countries also are obliged to make cuts in these areas, but theirs are not as large (for many, their levels of support were much lower to begin with), and are stretched over 10 years rather than six. But these cuts still leave agriculture a more protected sector than almost any other; average tariffs remain relatively high at around 40 per cent. And some countries employ "megatariffs" of up to 350 per cent to protect certain products.

Despite reductions in export subsidies and domestic farm programs, the Agreement on Agriculture allows continued support for certain policies designated as falling within the "green box." These include agro-environmental policies with insignificant impacts on production or trade, such as support for research, disaster payments and structural adjustment programs. In addition, the Agreement has exceptions under a "blue box" for direct payments made under production-limiting programs. One of the key issues for future negotiations is the scope of these exceptions. Some countries point out that agriculture is "multifunctional"—that sustainably practiced it not only produces food products, but also protects biodiversity, conserves soil, ensures national food security and so on. They argue that these social benefits should be paid for by the state, and that the resulting support payments belong in the green box. Critics charge that the multifunctionality argument is old wine in new bottles—that countries which did not want to stop supporting their agricultural sector have hit upon a new way to do so.

In a number of countries producers are increasingly using genetically modified organisms in agriculture. Environmental concerns over using GMOs have included, among others, the possibility that the insect- or herbicide-resistant traits of GMOs will spread to other less desirable plant varieties or that they pose unknown risks to human health by containing, for example, allergy- or cancer-causing substances. Others are concerned about GMOs being controlled by a relatively small number of companies and the possible implications for consumers and small-scale agricultural producers, particularly in developing countries. A number of issues could involve GMOs in trade. Conflicts over GMOs could lead to reduced market share if they are stopped at the border by importers. And, the potential disruption of trade flows in agriculture causes problems for less developed countries seeking to use GMOs to explore a potential for enhanced food production. This is an issue that will no doubt be addressed in the coming years, either by the WTO or the Biosafety Protocol of the Convention on Biological Diversity, or both.

5.7   Intellectual property rights

The WTO's Agreement on Trade-Related Aspects of Intellectual Property Rights sets out the kind of protection that different kinds of innovation should receive (for example, books must be protected by copyrights, industrial processes must be covered by patents), and holds all WTO members to the same minimum standard of protection. The Agreement is unique among the WTO rules in that it is *positively proscriptive*. That is, all other WTO rules describe what countries should not do, whereas TRIPS describes what countries *should* do.

Intellectual property rights are patents, copyrights or other means of protecting an innovator's exclusive ability to control the use of his or her innovation for a specified period. During that time the intellectual property rights holder will usually try to market and sell the idea, seeking to recoup his or her investment in research and development. Intellectual property rights trade off the welfare of the innovator, whose efforts deserve compensation, against the welfare of society at large, which would benefit by having unlimited access to the innovation. For sustainable development, properly balancing that trade-off is crucial. Innovations, whether in energy efficiency, new medicines or improved agricultural varieties, are at the heart of sustainable development, but they do little good unless they are widely disseminated.

How do strong intellectual property rights, such as the WTO TRIPS Agreement, affect that balance? On the plus side, they may help ensure that more innovation will take place. Without the guarantee of such protection, who would bother to spend millions of dollars developing, for example, new software or new drugs, which could then be copied at will by others and distributed at minimal costs? (Intellectual property tends to have very high costs of development, but low costs of reproduction once developed.)

Strong intellectual property rights also help new technologies—the products of innovation—get disseminated. Technology transfer is usually a commercial venture, and happens through a number of means:

- Direct investment (for example, building a factory);
- Joint ventures with domestic firms;
- Wholly owned subsidiaries;
- Licensing (selling the rights to use the technology);
- Training and information exchanges; and,
- Sales and management contracts.

Innovators will be more comfortable using these mechanisms in countries that are obliged to enforce strong protection of intellectual property rights. That obligation assures them that their innovations will not be freely pirated. So strong intellectual property rights increase the willingness of firms to disseminate their technologies in countries that adopt them.

On the negative side, TRIPS-style protection of intellectual property rights can have a number of undesirable effects. First, if it is too strong, it tilts the balance too far toward the innovator. Critics of the TRIPS Agreement argue that its long terms of protection—20 years for patents and other intellectual property rights—over-reward the intellectual property rights holders, and punish the public by keeping the protected good too expensive for too long. Overly strong protection may thus slow down the spread of new technologies. Improperly applied, it may also stifle innovation; section 5.7.2 on agriculture gives examples of how this might work. Finally, TRIPS-style protection may work against sustainable development objectives by making goods such as pharmaceuticals more costly and less accessible to the poor. Several developing countries, when implementing TRIPS, have had to dismantle domestic industries based on cheap copying of foreign-patented drugs, forcing up prices dramatically. Patents in some of those countries used to protect only the process used to make a product, not the product itself, so it was legally possible to make the same drug in a slightly different way without paying royalties. But TRIPS demands *product* patents as well as *process* patents, putting an end to this kind of production.

Recognizing the potential negative effects from granting intellectual property rights, TRIPS contains an exception whereby WTO members are not obliged to grant patents for products or processes where "the prevention within [national] territory of [their] commercial exploitation . . . is necessary to protect *ordre public* [law and order] or morality, including to protect human, animal or plant life or health or to avoid serious prejudice to the environment."

This may be an important exception for the environment but it is not well defined, never having been tested.

The sections that follow will examine the implications of intellectual property rights and the TRIPS Agreement for efforts to preserve biodiversity, and to promote sustainable agriculture.

5.7.1 TRIPS and the Convention on Biological Diversity

The CBD requires parties to co-operate to ensure that patents and other intellectual property rights "are supportive of and do not run counter to" its objectives, implicitly recognizing the potential for conflict. The main potential problems stem from the CBD's emphasis on ensuring that local and indigenous communities—mainly in developing countries—have control over and reap a share of the benefits from their own biodiversity-related traditional knowledge and "informal" innovations. An example of traditional knowledge is the oral history held by an indigenous community of the herbs and plants that have medicinal properties—information of great value to pharmaceutical researchers searching for new drugs. Informal innovation is innovation that is carried out by the actual user of the product or system. For example, farmers have traditionally created innovative new plant varieties by saving seed from previous crops, selecting and planting, generation after generation, those that perform best under their local conditions.

This kind of knowledge and innovation has immense and growing value. Genetic resources provide the foundation for a range of new products and technological applications in biotechnology, agriculture, medicine and other areas. Knowledge developed and held in traditional knowledge systems of indigenous and local communities can provide clues to genetic resources or biochemicals that can be used for pharmaceuticals, herbal medicines and other products. They can also provide new genetic material for plant breeders, allowing them to confer desired traits such as pest and drought resistance to crop plants. In one case alone, incorporating disease resistance from a Latin American corn variety spared U.S. corn crops from devastation and saved the industry an estimated $6 billion.

Informal innovation and traditional knowledge do not get equal treatment under the TRIPS Agreement. TRIPS emphasizes patents and other intellectual property rights defined under conventional intellectual property regimes. These are almost all held in the developed countries by inventors and corporations in the formal research sector. No mechanisms are spelled out that grant traditional communities control over their knowledge and innovations, or that ensure they reap a share of the benefits therefrom. This treatment fails to deliver the kinds of incentives recognized by the CBD as essential to helping preserve biodiversity. Local communities will have much more reason to help preserve biodiversity if they derive some income from it.

TRIPS, however, does not require national intellectual property rights regimes to be identical. Individual countries have the right to adopt *higher* standards than TRIPS requires, and they can address concerns related to the CBD by imposing certain requirements on the process of applying for intellectual property rights protection, such as certification of origin. Countries can also create mechanisms within intellectual property rights law to achieve specific objectives, such as benefit sharing.

5.7.2 TRIPS and agriculture

Strengthening any system of intellectual property rights raises all the stakes because the protection it gives to innovation makes investment in research and development potentially much more profitable. For agriculture, this dynamic creates two troubling side-effects.

The first is that the increasing returns to investment have helped shape an industry structure where bigger is better. Without strong intellectual property protection it would be impossible to invest the tens of millions of dollars necessary to bring new products to market. But since such investments are profitable only the big will survive. This reality has led to a significant concentration of ownership in the seed industry, with those firms capable of very large investments increasingly buying out smaller firms to consolidate their market positions. One of the first results is likely to be higher prices for products based on intellectual property such as seeds, since there will be less price competition between the few remaining firms.

A second concern is the rapidly shrinking genetic diversity of cultivated species, as farmers switch from traditional varieties to new high-yielding strains developed by professional breeders. Beginning decades ago in the Green Revolution, farmers began to turn away from traditional varieties and to adopt modern strains that promised better yields and better resistance to pests and disease. By providing incentives to breeders to develop the new improved varieties, strengthened intellectual property rights contribute to this decline in diversity, although they are only one of a host of contributing factors.

TRIPS contains an exemption that allows WTO members to refuse to grant patents for plants and animals (other than micro-organisms). But if members wish to deny patents to plants, they must protect them by some "effective *sui generis* regime"—a system specially designed for a certain type of intellectual property—or a combination of the two systems.

The drafters of the TRIPS Agreement undoubtedly had in mind the International Convention for the Protection of New Varieties of Plants (UPOV Convention)—a regime that many countries are using. But some developing countries are creating their own *sui generis* systems, citing aspects of UPOV on which they want to improve (see Box 5-3). In the mandated review of the TRIPS Agreement in the WTO (starting in 2000), many developed countries are expected to push for less flexibility to develop such regimes.

Box 5-3: UPOV (1991) and sustainable development

Some argue that three elements of UPOV's 1991 Act may conflict with sustainable development objectives:

1. Duration of protection: Twenty years of protection, which may be too long from a consumer's perspective.

2. Breeders' exemption: Limited scope for breeders' exemption— the traditional free access of breeders to protected material for research purposes. If the new variety is "essentially derived" from the original variety, the intellectual property rights must be shared with the original innovator.

3. Farmers' rights vs. breeders' rights: Strong protection of breeders' rights—the intellectual property rights of formal innovators—but no protection of farmers' rights—the intellectual property rights of informal (typically poor) innovators.

If patents are used to protect plant varieties, they may in fact stifle innovation. Traditionally, innovation has been based on existing varieties which scientists used for improvements, and for which a breeders' exemption (the right to use protected varieties in their research and claim ownership of the results) has been granted. But patents don't provide for a breeders' exemption, and researchers will have to pay for access to patented materials used in their research, if they are allowed access at all. Also, many firms engage in 'patent stacking'—taking out patents for different aspects of a single innovation, forcing several royalty applications and payments. Finally, trends in patent applications allowing for broadly defined patents based on plant characteristics, rather than on the genes that produced those characteristics, may discourage further research. Patents have been granted, for example, for such broad categories as sunflower seeds with high oleic acid content. To the extent that such a patent stifles innovative research into improved ways of producing high oleic acid sunflowers, strong intellectual property rights protection defeats one of its main avowed goals.

5.8 Investment

The links between investment and trade in goods covered by GATT, TBT and other WTO agreements are straightforward: trade in goods can lead to investment.

As a foreign producer gains a greater share of a national market, it may make sense to invest and sell locally rather than continue to export from abroad. Investment in a foreign country is often based on the expectation of trade, including the possibility of importing goods to the investor's home country. The links are even stronger where trade in services is concerned. Indeed, the General Agreement on Trade in Services, concluded as part of the Uruguay Round, contains quite extensive provisions on investment under the heading of "right of establishment."

Some countries wanted to include investment in the Uruguay Round, but were unable to get broad agreement to do so. The result was a very narrow agreement focusing on trade-related investment measures known as the TRIMs Agreement. The question of including investment in further negotiations is again on the table, with the European Union and Japan advocating this approach. And, compared with what it was during the Uruguay Round, the resistance from developing countries is now less energetic.

The international debate about investment has long been polarized. One group of countries—generally, those from the OECD—has sought to promote an agreement on investor rights and their protection. In UNCTAD another group of countries has sought to develop rules governing investor obligations. Nowhere have both aspects been treated together.

Investment is vital to the prospects for sustainable development. The ultimate goal of policies to promote sustainable development is to transform the structure of economies by supporting sustainable activities and discouraging unsustainable ones. Many current activities, and most of our production technologies, are known to be unsustainable and will need to be modified or replaced. But to do so will require large investments, and, in particular, the most efficient use of limited capital resources. An appropriately structured international investment agreement could help to achieve these aims.

After the successful conclusion of the Uruguay Round, an attempt was made to negotiate a Multilateral Agreement on Investment within the OECD. The draft MAI was modelled on GATT and on many bilateral investment agreements. It provided for a range of investor rights and for a dispute settlement process to protect them. Purposely, the MAI remained ambiguous in its institutional provisions to facilitate its ultimate transfer into the WTO.

But MAI negotiations were called off after broadly based environmental opposition had drawn attention to the draft's shortcomings and after several other interests had joined in opposing the draft MAI. Moreover, as negotiations neared their end, countries sought so many exceptions to the disciplines imposed by the MAI that it was rendered much less meaningful.

The problems with an investment agreement go beyond the environmental objections that were raised. Productive investment is a long-term activity.

Facilities built today may still exist a century later, albeit in much modified form. Moreover, foreign investors, unlike traders, acquire extensive rights in the host country—for example, the right to employ people, to use environmental resources, to benefit from infrastructure, to transport, export and import. An investment agreement must balance investor rights with investor responsibilities at all stages of the investment process. That requires a regime with characteristics that differ markedly from those of the GATT/WTO regime, which deals with the discrete activity of a good or service entering a country. In particular it must be able to make case-by-case discretionary judgments in a broad framework. In other words, whereas an investment regime must be rules-based, like the trade regime, it must also be more dynamic and more willing to engage in discussion with states and investors.

5.9   Government procurement

Government procurement is government purchases of goods and services—everything from office supplies to jet fighters to consultants. Government expenditures typically make up a large portion of GDP—10 to 25 per cent in OECD countries—and what governments decide to buy or not buy can have an enormous influence on the economy and environment. This fact has led many governments to begin thinking about how to green their procurement, making it a force for environmental protection, or at least reduced environmental damage.

Most such schemes to date have involved either a price preference for goods that meet certain criteria (for example, recycled paper can be up to 10 per cent more costly and will still be bought), or a specification of the product's attributes (for example, all government fleet automobiles must have a certain fuel efficiency). Because they are administratively simple (though not for the purchasing agents), they can make a real difference, and because they portray the government favourably in the public eye, such schemes will undoubtedly be increasingly popular.

The greening of government procurement may have trade implications. Many of the issues are the same as those posed by labelling and certification schemes (see section 5.4). The purchasing requirements may be based on process and production method standards—for example, governments may give preference to goods made that release little carbon into the atmosphere. Or they may simply require a domestic-level ecolabel or environmental management certification, saving purchasing officers the trouble of verification and auditing. But, as with labelling, the PPM criteria set in one country may not always be relevant in another. And the specifications may be, intentionally or unintentionally, set up in ways that favour domestic producers. Labelling and certification dealt with voluntary standards, and so there was some debate over whether they were in fact covered by the existing trade rules. But if a government requires that all the paper it buys be certified by a domestic ecolabel, we enter the grey area between voluntary standards and mandatory technical regulations.

The WTO's Government Procurement Agreement is different from most of the WTO agreements, in that it is *plurilateral*. This means that countries do not automatically subscribe by being WTO members, and in fact only a few currently do. The GPA currently has some 30 signatories, mostly from OECD countries. The focus of the Agreement is to force governments to tender bids for their purchases transparently and fairly.

Unlike GATT, the GPA does not prohibit discrimination among like products, but rather focuses on discrimination between foreign and domestic suppliers. It does demand, though, that any requirements should not be "prepared, adopted or applied with a view to, or with the effect of, creating unnecessary obstacles to international trade"—a requirement that has yet to be interpreted. It also mandates that technical specifications should be "based on international standards, where such exist; otherwise, on national technical regulations, recognized national standards, or building codes." A national technical regulation, according to the footnote that modifies this text, is any standard set by a recognized body. ISO 14001 presumably fits this bill, and, arguably, so would most national-level ecolabelling programs.

For now these issues are on the horizon. The greening of government procurement is a recent phenomenon. And the GPA is in an uncertain state; WTO members may strengthen it through further negotiations, but no consensus has been reached on the need to do so any time soon. And the Agreement has yet to be interpreted by a dispute settlement body in a way that would clarify how it might treat PPM-based discrimination.

5.10 MEAs and the WTO

According to Agenda 21, international trade and environmental laws should be mutually supportive. Nowhere is this challenge greater than in the relationship between the WTO disciplines and the trade provisions of multilateral environmental agreements.

Of the 200 or so MEAs currently in existence, over 20 incorporate trade measures to achieve their goals. This means that the agreements use restraints on trade in particular substances or products, either between parties to the treaty or between parties and non-parties, or both. Although this is a relatively small number of MEAs, they are some of the most important: the 1975 Convention on International Trade in Endangered Species of Flora and Fauna (CITES), the 1987 Montreal Protocol on Substances that Deplete the Ozone Layer, the

1992 Basel Convention on the Control of Transboundary Movement of Hazardous Wastes and their Disposal, and the Cartagena Biosafety Protocol to the 1993 Convention on Biological Diversity (see Box 2-3). As well, the Convention on the Control of Persistent Organic Pollutants, currently under negotiation, will certainly contain trade measures.

Trade-restricting measures in an environmental agreement may serve either of two purposes (see the more complete discussion of this topic in section 2.4.4). First, they may control trade itself, where trade is perceived to be the source of environmental damage that the convention seeks to address. CITES, which requires import and export licences for trade in endangered species, is a good example. Another is the Rotterdam PIC Convention, which calls on parties to notify other parties before certain types of exports, and allows parties to ban some imports.

Second, trade-restricting measures play two types of enforcement roles. They provide an additional incentive to join and adhere to the MEA by barring non-parties from trading in restricted goods with parties. If you are not a party to the Basel Convention, for example, you cannot ship waste to or import waste from any of the parties. And these measures help ensure the MEA's effectiveness, again by restricting trade with non-parties. This prevents "leakage," where non-parties simply increase production of the restricted good and ship it to the parties that have restricted their own production. The Montreal Protocol, for example, bans trade with non-parties in ozone-depleting substances and products containing them, a provision that many observers agree was crucial to the wide international support the Protocol has achieved. It is difficult to see these kinds of enforcement roles being filled without trade measures.

The problem is that such measures may conflict with WTO rules. Chapter 3 described the obligations of WTO members to observe the most-favoured nation and national-treatment principles, as well as provisions on eliminating quantitative restrictions (Articles I, III and XI). An agreement that says parties can use trade restrictions against some countries (non-parties) but not against others (parties) may violate all three articles. It discriminates between otherwise "like" products based on their country of origin, it imposes quantitative restrictions, and it may treat imported goods differently from "like" domestic goods.

Such trade-restricting measures might be used in two ways. First, a party could use them against another party (for example, the prior informed consent system of the Rotterdam Convention is used just among parties to the Convention). Most analysts argue that this is not a problem, since both countries have voluntarily agreed to be bound by the MEA's rules, including the use of trade measures. This may be true where the trade measures in question are spelled out in the agreement, but problems may arise where the agreement just spells out objectives, and leaves it to the parties to make domestic laws to achieve them. Parties to the Kyoto Protocol, for example, may fulfill their obligations (spelled out in the Protocol) to lower greenhouse gas emissions by any number of trade-restrictive measures (*not* spelled out). Although WTO members have expressed hope that disputes between parties might be settled within the MEAs themselves, a party complaining about the use of such *non-specific trade measures* would almost certainly choose to take its case to the WTO.

Second, a party could use trade measures against a non-party, where both are WTO members. Here, the non-party has *not* voluntarily agreed to be subjected to the MEA's trade measures. As with party-to-party measures the trade-restricting party may be violating the non-party's rights under WTO rules, but here the non-party might take the matter to the WTO even if the measures are spelled out specifically in the MEA. To date no WTO or GATT dispute of this type has arisen. The spectre of a potential conflict, however, has generated considerable concern in the environment and trade communities. As well as threatening the integrity of existing MEAs, the potential for conflict with WTO rules is a near deal-breaking concern in new MEA negotiations, as demonstrated by the difficulties in drafting the Biosafety Protocol, the Kyoto Protocol and the Rotterdam Convention.

The WTO is addressing this issue in the CTE, where it has been on the agenda since the Committee's 1995 inception. Three types of proposals have surfaced:

1. To interpret the general exceptions of Article XX to create a 'window' for MEAs;

2. To seek WTO waivers for MEAs case by case; and,

3. To draw up lists of criteria or guidelines that trade measures would have to meet to be considered acceptable.

Some countries also suggested that the status quo was sufficient to deal with the problems of potential conflict.

So far it has been impossible to reach agreement. Some countries are concerned that the window approach would set dangerous precedents for other social issues and open the WTO to protectionism. The waiver approach has been criticized for failing to provide certainty and guidance to MEA negotiators. And both the waiver approach and the criteria approach seem too much like trade policy-makers passing judgment on international environmental law (some MEAs are older and have more members than the WTO). Some of these criticisms are blunted by proposals that incorporate elements of more than one approach.

In the end it is clearly in the interest of both the environment and trade communities to find a solution to the potential conflicts between the two regimes of law.

Suggested readings

Environmental standards and PPMs

OECD. *Process and production methods: Conceptual framework and considerations on use of PPM-based trade measures* (OCDE/GD(97)137). Paris: OECD, 1997. <http://www.olis.oecd.org/olis/1997doc.nsf/linkto/ocde-gd(97)137>.

von Moltke, Konrad. "Reassessing 'like products'." Paper presented at Chatham House Conference, "Trade, Investment and the Environment," 29 & 30 October 1998. <http://iisd.ca/trade/pdf/likeproducts.pdf>.

Environmental standards and competitiveness

Jaffe, A. et al. "Environmental regulation and the competitiveness of U.S. manufacturing: What does the evidence tell us?" *Journal of Economic Literature* 33 (March 1995): 132–163.

UNCTAD. *Opportunities and constraints of internalizing environmental costs and benefits in prices of rubber and rubber goods.* Proceedings of an UNCTAD/International Rubber Study Group workshop, Manchester, UK, 13 June 1997. <http://www.unctad.org/trade_env/docs/manch-ws.pdf>.

Environmental standards, science and precaution

Raffensperger, Carolyn and Joel Tickner, eds. *Protecting public health and the environment: Implementing the precautionary principle.* Washington, D.C.: Island Press, 1999. <http://www.islandpress.org/ecocompass/prevent/index.html>.

von Moltke, Konrad. "The dilemma of the precautionary principle in international trade." *Bridges* 3, no. 6, (July-August 1999). <http://iisd.ca/pdf/precaution.pdf>.

Ecolabelling and EMS certification programs

van Dyke, Brennan and Charles Arden-Clarke. *ISO eco-labelling standards, the WTO and MEAs: A legal briefing examining elements of DIS 14020.* Gland, Switzerland: WWF International, 1997.

IISD. *Global green standards: ISO 14000 and sustainable development.* Winnipeg: IISD, 1996. <http://iisd.ca/greenstand/default.htm>.

Lehtonen, Markku. *Criteria in environmental labelling: A comparative analysis of environmental criteria in selected labelling schemes* (environment and trade series #13). Geneva: UNEP, 1997.

OECD. *Eco-labelling: Actual effects of selected programmes* (OCDE/GD(97)105). Paris: OECD, 1997. <http://www.olis.oecd.org/olis/1997doc.nsf/linkto/ocde-gd(97)105>.

UNCTAD. *Report of the expert meeting on possible trade and investment impacts of environmental management standards, particularly the ISO 14000 series, on developing countries, and opportunities and needs in this context* (TD/B/COM.1/10, TD/B/COM.1EM.4/3). Geneva: UNCTAD, 1997. <http://www.uncatd.org/en/special/c1em4d3.htm>.

Zarilli, Simonetta, Veena Jha and René Vossenaar. *Eco-labelling and international trade.* New York: St. Martin's Press, 1997.

Subsidies

IISDnet Subsidy Watch. IISD. <http://iisd.ca/subsidywatch/default.htm>.

Meyers, Norman with Jennifer Kent. *Perverse subsidies: Tax dollars undercutting our economies and environments alike.* Winnipeg: IISD, 1998. <http://iisd.ca/about/prodcat/govern.htm#perverse>.

Porter, Gareth. *Fisheries subsidies, overfishing and trade* (environment and trade series #16). Geneva: UNEP, 1998.

Steenblik, Ronald. *Previous multilateral efforts to discipline subsidies to natural resource based industries.* Paper prepared for the Pacific Economic Co-operation Council Workshop on the Impact of Government Financial Transfers on Fisheries Management, Resource Sustainability, and International Trade, Manila, Philippines, 17-19 August 1998. <http://economics.iucn.org/pdf/issues-01-03.pdf>.

Agriculture

Government of Norway. *Non-trade concerns in a multifunctional agriculture: Implications for agricultural policy and the multilateral trading system.* Oslo: Ministry of Agriculture, 1998. <http://www.dep.no/ld/landbruk/faktorare.html>.

Murphy, Sophia. *Trade and food security: An assessment of the Uruguay Round Agreement on Agriculture.* London: Catholic Institute for International Relations, 1999. <http://www.ciir.org/ipd/fs.html>.

WWF International. *Directing WTO negotiations towards sustainable agriculture and rural development*. Gland: WWF International, 1999. <http://www.panda.org/resources/publications/sustainability/wto-papers/wto-sard.html>.

Intellectual property rights

Cosbey, Aaron. *Sustainable development effects of the WTO TRIPS Agreement: A focus on developing countries*. Winnipeg: IISD, 1996. <http://iisd.ca/trade/trips.htm>.

Downes, David. *Integrating implementation of the CBD and the rules of the WTO*. Gland: IUCN, 1999.

Dutfield, Graham. *Intellectual property rights, trade and biodiversity*. London: Earthscan/IUCN, 1999.

South Centre. *The TRIPS Agreement: A guide for the South*. Geneva: South Centre, 1997. <http://www.southcentre.org/publications/trips/tripsmain.pdf (main text)> and <http://www.southcentre.org/publications/trips/tripsannexe.pdf (annex)>.

Investment

South Centre. *Foreign direct investment, development and the new global economic order*. Geneva: South Centre, 1997. <http://www.southcentre.org/publications/fdi/fdi.pdf>.

von Moltke, Konrad. *An international investment regime? Issues of sustainability*. Winnipeg: IISD, 2000. <http://iisd.ca/trade/pdf/investment.pdf>.

Ward, Halina and Duncan Brack, eds. *Trade, investment and the environment*. London: Royal Institute of International Affairs/Earthscan, 1999.

Government procurement

OECD. *Trade issues in the greening of public purchasing* (COM/TD/ENV (97)111/FINAL). Paris: OECD, 1997. <http://www.olis.oecd.org/olis/1997 doc.nsf/LINKTO/com-td-env(97)111-final>.

MEAs and the WTO

Brack, Duncan. "Reconciling the GATT and MEAs with trade provisions: The latest debate," *Review of European Community & International Environmental Law* 6, no. 2 (1997): 112–120.

Charnovitz, Steve. "MEAs and trade rules," *Environmental Policy and Law* 26, no. 4 (1996): 163–169.

OECD. *Trade measures in multilateral environmental agreements: Synthesis report of three case studies* (COM/ENV/TD(98)127/FINAL). Paris: OECD, 1998. <http://appli1.oecd.org/olis/1998doc.nsf/LinkTo/com-env-td(98)127-final>.

Stilwell, Matthew and Elizabeth Turk. *Trade measures and multilateral environmental agreements: Resolving uncertainty and removing the WTO chill factor*. Gland: WWF International, 1999.

UNEP. *The use of trade measures in selected MEAs* (environment and trade series #10). Geneva: UNEP, 1996. <http://www.unep.ch/trade.html>.

–6–
Institutional issues

THE PREVIOUS CHAPTERS ANALYZED THE LINKAGES between environment and trade from a physical and economic as well as a legal and policy perspective. A number of institutional questions also arise when we attempt to address the relationship between trade and the environment. Making trade and environment mutually supportive may require changing the existing institutions to accommodate new concerns, or building new ones. This chapter looks at mechanisms for openness in trade policy-making at the national and multilateral levels, and at the possible emergence of a new set of institutions to review trade liberalization agreements.

6.1   Openness in trade policy-making

Openness consists of two basic elements: first, timely, easy and full access to information for all those affected; and second, public participation in the decision-making process. Openness is widely recognized as being valuable to government, since it makes bureaucracies more responsive and accountable, and can bring more and better information to the decision-making process. The result of open practice is better decisions, particularly in areas with widespread impacts such as trade, environment and development policies.

Openness in making trade policy is important for environmental concerns on at least two levels. The first is at the domestic level. The ideal scenario would be for all concerned stakeholders to be informed and consulted as governments seek to define their national interests. The results of these deliberations would inform the positions taken by the country's trade negotiators.

At the multilateral level two major areas of interest are the WTO's document derestriction policies and the dispute settlement mechanisms. A WTO decision in 1996 measurably improved document derestriction from what it had been. And the WTO has constructed an exceptional Web site with access to all derestricted documents. In the lead up to the WTO's 1999 Seattle Ministerial Conference, the negotiating positions submitted by all WTO members were featured on the site, something that would have been inconceivable even a few years ago. But a number of important restrictions still remain in effect (see Box 6-1).

Box 6-1: Document derestriction in the WTO

All WTO documents are derestricted except for the following:

- Any document submitted by a member who requests that it be restricted.

- All working documents (draft budgets, proposals, reports): these are considered for derestriction when the relevant report, proposal or item is adopted, or six months after circulation, whichever is sooner. Working documents from certain bodies are treated differently, and are considered for derestriction on a regular six-month cycle.

- Minutes of meetings of any WTO body (except those of the Trade Policy Review Mechanism): these are considered for derestriction six months after circulation.

- Reports of dispute resolution panels: unless a party to the dispute asks for a delay, these are derestricted 10 days after circulation.

- The arguments that members submit to dispute resolution panels.

The dispute settlement procedures are an area of special interest; a number of environment-related trade disputes have gone through the procedures since they were established in 1995. The rules here are restrictive by the normal standards of international law: The arguments that the parties submit to the panels are restricted, in effect closing the process to public scrutiny until a judgment has been rendered. It may not be completely closed from public participation, however; the recent shrimp-turtle Appellate Body decision chose to consider unsolicited briefs submitted by non-governmental organizations. It may be that this decision will set a precedent for accepting the so-called *amicus curiae* (friends of the court) briefs. But critics have argued that the usefulness of such briefs is compromised if the intervenors are not allowed to read the arguments of the parties to the dispute.

Openness at the domestic and multilateral levels are linked in two ways. First, policies at the multilateral level that restrict documents may impair the ability of the public to make meaningful contributions to the debates at the national level. Second, the resistance to openness at the multilateral level by some states has occurred in part because their domestic-level processes are relatively closed, and they are wary of granting more rights to the public at the multilateral level than they grant their own nationals.

6.2 Environmental assessment of trade agreements

Before countries send their negotiators into trade talks, they first do their best to understand how the different negotiating scenarios will play out in their domestic economies. In which sectors should they be fighting hard for reduced tariffs, and in which should they be striving to maintain protection? Without an idea of where their interests lie, based on an assessment of potential economic impacts, they would be negotiating without having the full picture.

The same logic underlies the idea of environmental assessment of trade liberalization agreements. A country's well-being is not only affected by the *economic* impacts of trade agreements, but also by how such agreements affect the environmental and social structures, thus the growing interest in an assessment which considers the implications for the environment (see Box 6-2). Perhaps the greatest value of environmental assessments in identifying problems and possibilities is that they bring a wide variety of perspectives to the analysis, including those of non-trade governmental ministries, and non-governmental organizations with expertise in environmental and social issues. The scope, boundaries and focus of such assessments, however, will have to be determined by countries based on their development priorities and other environmental and socio-economic considerations.

Box 6-2: Environmental assessments of trade agreements in practice

- In 1993 the OECD Ministerial Council recommended that "governments should examine or review trade and environmental policies and agreements with potentially significant effects on the other policy area early in their development to assess the implications for the other policy area and to identify alternative policy options for addressing concerns."

- The U.S. and Canada undertook assessments of the environmental impacts of both NAFTA and the Uruguay Round, and are undertaking *ex ante* (forward-looking) assessments of possible future negotiations.

- The North American Commission for Environmental Cooperation assessed the environmental effects of NAFTA.

- The EU commissioned a "sustainability impact assessment" of its negotiating position for the proposed Millennium Round of trade negotiations. If a round does occur other countries are likely to do the same.

- An increasing number of environmental economists are undertaking independent assessments of liberalization in particular sectors.

Environmental assessments grow out of an established legal institution in many countries, where it is required to conduct environmental reviews of certain types of projects and policies. In some countries the procedures to be followed in such reviews are spelled out in great detail. Usually, they will include extensive participation from the public as part of the process.

A number of options are available for the timing of such assessments. They can be conducted before negotiations take place, to help shape negotiating positions. They can occur continually during negotiations. Or they can occur after the negotiations have finished, to try to identify the effects of a concluded agreement. In fact, all three options are different exercises and serve to complement each other.

Assessments often strive to identify not only potential problems, but also policies that could address those problems. These might be so-called "flanking" measures—complementary policies or measures to mitigate expected impacts, such as increased environmental protection. They might also be safeguards built into the liberalization agreement itself. Or they might be modifications to the proposed scope or depth of liberalization.

The challenges of conducting thorough environmental or sustainability assessments are enormous. Very few, if any, countries have adequate environmental data. And even with such data in hand, analysts then need to model how trade liberalization has impacts on the economy, and how environmental effects flow from those economic changes. If the analysis is expanded from an environmental to a sustainable development focus, we add another layer of complexity. How do we bring in such key variables as income distribution, health, nutrition, education and urban migration? Despite the complexities, sustainability assessments will probably continue to be undertaken and refined, since a blurred vision of the future is better than none at all.

Suggested readings

Openness in trade policy-making

Charnovitz, Steve. "Participation of NGOs in the WTO." *University of Pennsylvania Journal of International Economic Law* 17, no. 1 (1996): 331–357.

Enders, Alice. *Openness in the WTO.* Winnipeg: IISD, 1998. <http://iisd.ca/trade/knopen.htm>.

Esty, Daniel. *Why the WTO needs environmental NGOs.* Geneva: International Centre for Trade and Sustainable Development, 1997. <http://www.ictsd.org/English/esty.pdf>.

Environmental assessment of trade agreements

Commission for Environmental Cooperation. *Assessing environmental effects of the NAFTA: An analytic framework (Phase II) and issue studies.* Montreal: CEC, 1999. <http://www.cec.org/english/resources/publications/eandt6.cfm?format=2>.

OECD. *Methodologies for environmental assessment of trade liberalisation agreements* (COM/TD/ENV(99)92/FINAL). Paris: OECD, 1999. <http://www.oecd.org/ech/26-27oct/docs/report.pdf>.

Sustainability impact assessment of proposed WTO new round of multilateral trade negotiations. Institute for Development Policy and Management, University of Manchester, UK, 1999. <http://fs2.idpm.man.ac.uk/sia/>.

WWF International. *Developing a methodology for the environmental assessment of trade liberalisation agreements.* Gland, Switzerland: WWF International, 1998. <http://www.panda.org/resources/publications/sustainability/wto-papers/method.html>.

–7–
Environmental aspects of regional trade agreements

THIS CHAPTER LOOKS AT three very different trade agreements—NAFTA, the EU and Mercosur—to explore the different approaches each has adopted in addressing the issues of trade and environment.

7.1   The North American Free Trade Agreement

NAFTA is a trade agreement between Canada, Mexico and the United States, which entered into force January 1, 1994. NAFTA has side accords (separate non-trade agreements) on labour and the environment, without which it is doubtful the U.S. would have accepted the Agreement.

The environmental agreement created the Commission for Environmental Cooperation, which promotes environmental cooperation among the three countries, and by which dispute settlement provisions can be invoked if a country persistently fails to enforce environmental laws that have conferred a trade benefit. Note that the CEC itself does not set standards in the various countries, though part of its mandate is to help harmonize them upward. Rather, its role in such disputes is to see that enforcement of existing laws takes place. It is also charged with, among other things, monitoring the environmental effects of NAFTA.

7.1.1 Investment: Chapter 11

In NAFTA's Article 11 the parties promise that they will not try to attract investment by relaxing or ignoring domestic health, safety or environmental regulations. This is a laudable promise, but there is no enforcement mechanism to ensure that it is kept.

Other parts of Chapter 11 strive to ensure that foreign NAFTA investors will be safe from harassment by host governments. They do not allow expropriation without due process, for example, and in general oblige host governments to follow the same standards for foreign investors as they do for domestic ones.

Recent research has shown, however, that these provisions have been defined in unintended ways, and have been used to attack environmental laws in all three countries. Investors have filed a number of suits against the three governments—few of which have yet been settled—alleging that their investment interests are damaged by environmental regulations. In one case a U.S. firm argued that a Canadian ban on exports of PCBs (a cancer-causing hazardous waste) violated the principle of national treatment, since U.S. waste processors were deprived of a source of business while Canadian waste processors were not.

7.1.2 Standards: Chapters 7 and 9

NAFTA deals with sanitary and phytosanitary (SPS) measures in Chapter 7, and all other standards-related measures (SRM), including environmental standards, in Chapter 9. The two chapters outline how the parties should establish their respective levels of protection, set the standards which achieve those levels of protection, and base those standards on science.

For both kinds of standards, NAFTA gives parties the right to establish the levels of protection they find appropriate. But with SPS measures on non-human health issues, the parties must do a sort of cost-benefit analysis of the problem and the solutions, and are bound to enact the most cost-effective solution. All SPS measures must also avoid differences in levels of protection in different cases, where those differences result in discrimination against foreign-produced goods. A party could not, for example, set low levels of protection on the fruits that it grows, and high levels on those it must import.

Having established the appropriate level of protection, the parties must draft legislation to achieve it. The SPS text requires that any measure be "necessary" to achieve the level of protection the party has chosen. In the GATT/WTO, "necessary" was at one point held to mean "least-trade restrictive," a condition disliked by environmentalists and others. The U.S. claims that the parties agreed not to use this test, but there is no legal agreement to that effect.

NAFTA also specifies that the parties' standards should be "based on scientific principles." In practice, this means (according to the U.S. interpretation) that although science must be used to determine the risks posed by a product, regulators can then set the tolerable risk at any level they like. In other words, science is not used to choose the appropriate levels of protection—this is a public policy choice—but only to determine the risks, which are then in turn used to determine levels of protection.

The NAFTA standards text seems to incorporate a precautionary approach; Articles 907.3 of the SRM text and 715.4 of the SPS text allow parties to enact environment, health and safety measures even where scientific evidence is inadequate to assess risk.

7.1.3 International environmental agreements: Chapter 104

NAFTA Article 104 lists seven international environmental agreements, and agrees that they will trump NAFTA in the case of disagreement. The seven IEAs are the following:

- The Montreal Protocol;

- The Basel Convention (when all three parties have ratified);

- CITES; and

- Four bilateral treaties.

This seems a step in the right direction—how to deal with IEAs is a topic of great controversy in the WTO. But NAFTA parties are all signatories to these agreements, and much of the WTO controversy is over disputes between signatories and non-signatories.

And then there is the fine print. The domestic laws resulting from these IEAs must be those "least inconsistent with the other provisions of [NAFTA]." So a party would have to show that a challenged measure could not have been somehow "better," or more consistent with NAFTA. But the more NAFTA-consistent alternative does not need to be politically or economically feasible.

7.2   The European Union

The European Union is the most highly evolved international organization. It is the product of more than 40 years of effort to integrate the countries of Europe economically and politically. Beginning with six members in 1954 and restricted to the coal and steel sectors of the economy, the EU now encompasses 15 members, all major aspects of economic policy as well as many related policy areas. Including yet more members is foreseen. At the heart of the EU is a customs union—and now a single market—with a common external tariff. It is a supranational organization, widely interpreted as providing for the shared exercise of its member states' sovereignty.

The EU can legislate in the sense that it can adopt binding legal instruments through the action of its institutions alone. For this purpose it has a complex institutional structure, involving legislative, executive, judicial and advisory organs. Most important among these are the Council—the ultimate legislative authority made up of representatives of the member states, the directly elected European Parliament which shares legislative responsibility, the Commission as executive organ, and the European Court of Justice.

The EU has two principal legislative instruments, the Regulation and the Directive. Regulations are directly applicable and are used for technical aspects of issues where the EU has exclusive competence—for example, trade or adjusting agricultural prices. Directives are the instrument of choice for most environmental issues since they determine the objectives to be achieved but leave member states free to choose the means of implementing them. In practice, directives can be technically quite detailed in those areas where upward harmonization is sought.

As the EU expanded its legislative reach internally it has also acquired the external responsibility for the areas subject to European legislation. As a result, the EU and its member states engage in a complex internal negotiating process before any international negotiations. In principle this process takes place in the Council, but a specialized body prepares Council decisions on trade: the Article 133 Committee. In international negotiations often the boundary shifts between those areas that fall into the responsibility of member states, those that are the exclusive domain of the EU, or those that are shared between them.

Within the WTO, the EU speaks with a single voice on all commercial policy matters. Because GATT originated as an administrative agreement rather than a formal international treaty, representation of the EU in the WTO falls to the executive organ of the EU, the Commission. As a result, individual member states of the EU have a limited role in the WTO but the EU as a whole is one of the two most important actors in the organization. No decisions can be taken without it.

The EU has developed extensive environmental legislation. As the shape of markets changes, essential market disciplines, including environmental requirements, must be adjusted to reflect the structure of integrated European markets. EU environmental legislation has more than 300 items, covering every aspect of environmental policy. Directives cover emission standards and quality objectives for water; managing hazardous and domestic waste; packaging; atmospheric emissions from plants and vehicles; air quality standards and the stratospheric ozone layer; all aspects of toxic substances control; nature protection, migratory birds, endangered species; wildlife; noise; and climate change. Furthermore, EU legislation addresses impact assessment, freedom of information, ecolabelling, eco-management and auditing, and has established financial and economic instruments for environmental management. The EU's Common Agricultural Policy provides substantial sums of money for protection of nature in rural areas.

Environmental management is a responsibility shared between the EU and member states, whereas trade lies exclusively with the EU. This asymmetry has rendered the balancing of environment and trade interests more difficult since the functions of key actors are different in the two areas of policy.

7.3 Mercosur

Mercosur—*Mercado Común del Sur* or the Southern Common Market—is a subregional integration agreement involving Brazil, Argentina, Uruguay and Paraguay, with Chile and Bolivia holding special associated status. It is now a customs union (all members have the same tariffs to the outside world) and is committed eventually to becoming a full common market. In this sense it aspires to regional integration like the EU, rather than a free trade area like NAFTA.

The Mercosur structure, though still evolving, provides several environment-related innovations. Mechanisms for public participation were provided in the original Protocol of *Ouro Preto*, through a *Foro Consultivo Economico y Social* or social and economic advisory council, which exists as part of the Mercosur institutional structure. This forum receives information from labour, business and consumer representatives. Experts from the public also attend relevant meetings of Mercosur's many technical subcommittees.

More explicit environment and trade linkages are made through various legal mechanisms that combine as elements of a developing regime. Several resolutions of the *Grupo Mercado Común* and decisions of the *Consejo de Mercado Común* have touched upon issues such as pesticides, energy policies and transport of hazardous products. In addition, meetings of the four countries' environment ministers laid a foundation for co-operation in the subregion on these issues. As a result, the Canela Declaration of 1992 created an informal working group, the *Reunion Especializada en Medio Ambiente*, to study environmental laws, standards and practices in the four countries. This forum evolved into the creation of a *Sub-Grupo No. 6* on the environment, which is one of the recognized technical working bodies of Mercosur. This group has discussed issues such as environment and competitiveness, non-tariff barriers to trade, and common systems of environmental information.

This body has been involved for over two years in negotiating a new environmental protocol, which is being added to the Treaty of Asuncion of Mercosur. A comprehensive stand-alone treaty, this draft agreement provides for upward harmonization of environmental management systems and increased co-operation on shared ecosystems, in addition to mechanisms for social participation. It includes provisions on instruments for environmental management, including quality standards, environmental impact assessment methods, environmental monitoring and costing, environmental information systems and certification processes. It also includes a section on protected areas, and one on conservation and sustainable use of natural resources, including biological diversity and proposed language on biosafety, wildlife, forests, soil, atmosphere and water conservation. It also includes provisions for protecting health and quality of life, social participation, regional co-operation and other general mechanisms for implementing the protocol. The regime is still evolving, and the challenge at hand is to ensure that the promise of the protocol does lead to effective regional co-operation and action on these issues and objectives.

Suggested readings

NAFTA

Mann, Howard and Konrad von Moltke. "NAFTA's Chapter 11 and the environment: Addressing the impacts of the investor-state process on the environment." Winnipeg: IISD, 1999. <http://iisd.ca/trade/chapter11.htm>

Johnston, Pierre Marc and Andre Beaulieu. *The environment and NAFTA: Understanding and implementing the new continental law.* New York: Island Press, 1996.

EU

von Moltke, Konrad. *The Maastricht Treaty and the Winnipeg principles on trade and sustainable development.* Winnipeg: IISD, 1995. <http://iisd.ca/pdf/maastricht.pdf>.

Mercosur

Tussie, Diana and Patricia Vasquez. "Regional integration and building blocks: The case of Mercosur," in Diana Tussie, ed., *The environment and international trade negotiations: Developing country stakes.* New York: IDRC/Macmillan Press, 1999.

–8–
Conclusion

The main goal of this handbook is to make the complex relationship between the environment and international trade more understandable and accessible to policy-makers, non-governmental organizations and the public. The book also aims to dispel the idea that the relationship between, trade, the environment and development can easily be described as either negative or positive. It is an immensely complex interaction that varies from country to country, sector to sector, and firm to firm. There are both threats and opportunities in this relationship for countries, local communities and firms pursuing economic development and environmental protection.

The challenge, for all these stakeholders, is to exploit the opportunities and reduce the threats, and in so doing to maximize the net positive contribution that trade can make to sustainable development. A broader and clearer understanding of the linkages between trade, environment and development among all stakeholders is a prerequisite for seizing those opportunities and reducing those threats.

The conclusions that can be drawn from this handbook are essentially about research and consensus-building, enhancement of international co-operation, and defining new and more balanced and participatory procedures for international policy-making on these issues. In particular, formal assessments of the environmental impacts of trade liberalization and the trade implications of environmental policies will have to be undertaken. These assessments will have to take account of the interrelated economic and social effects of environmental and trade policies, through integrated assessment techniques.

Research and assessment need to be undertaken in a participatory manner that includes all the relevant stakeholders. At the national level this implies involving civil society as well as government officials; at the international level this implies financial and technical assistance for developing countries and those with economies in transition to build their capacity to undertake this analysis. This assistance, and the broader awareness of the linkages it fosters, will help build consensus on the policy integration challenges that are faced, and the solutions that will then have to be developed at both national and international levels.

International negotiations which lead to new trade agreements will also have to be characterized by more balanced and equitable participation of developed and developing countries, if those agreements are to accurately reflect the needs and conditions in all countries. We also hope that an enhanced understanding and awareness of trade, environment and development linkages will inform implementation of existing, and negotiation of new, multilateral environmental agreements, enabling them better to respond to the needs and conditions in countries at differing levels of development.

Achieving these objectives requires first a broader understanding of the linkages between the environment and trade, and the policies designed to foster both. UNEP and IISD hope that this handbook will foster that broader understanding, and both organizations remain open to suggestions to improve the handbook in this regard, and offer their collaboration and partnership to the same end.

Index